You're a poet,
keep writing!
ᶜ Love,
Athena
&
Bambi

Went To Ralph's
To Get A Chicken

for Jack Grapes

The Los Angeles Poets & Writers Collective

BAMBAZ Press
Los Angeles 2016

Editors: Bambi Here, Marley Klaus, and Lee McCarthy
Cover Design: Baz Here
Cover Photo: Baz Here

ISBN:

BAMBAZ Press
www.bambazpress.com
fred@bambazpress.com
548 S Spring Street 1201
Los Angeles, California 90013 USA

Printed in the United States of America

From the editors

So, Jack. Yes. How could we not? In honor of your 75th,
we asked people to write something with this in it:
"So I went to Ralph's to get a chicken."
We, your brood, send this communal cluck in celebration of you,
with gratitude for all you've given us.

Lee McCarthy & Marley Klaus
Bambi Here & Baz Here
(...with assistance from Lisa Segal and Linda Neal)

CONTRIBUTORS

A SUPERMARKET OFF FAIRFAX

Tresha Haefner

What thoughts I have of you tonight, Jack Grapes,
for I drive under a melodious moon, disfeathering the feet of crows, on
my way to Ralphs, to buy a chicken.
Self-conscious and dreaming of grandeur
I shop for a few ears of corn to hear my sighs,
I dream of your large eyes, the tar pit where so many have thrown
the bones of their newly spoken words.
And now I find aisles full of mulberries, mulling over their lost mothers,
muses lifting apples out of the bins, buying cereal, seducing the butcher,
and hunting down the boy who would bring them
their baskets full of bread.
And you, Bukowski. What were you doing down by the peaches?
Abandoning your stroller full of beer? The writing desk you kept so clean?
I saw you too Jack Grapes, peeling grapes
between the babes in the frozen food aisle,
asking questions of each, "Where is the chicken?" "What price bananas?"
"Will you be my Mississippi after the moon has frozen me cold?"
Between meat and produce, a flock of unhatched chicks
left their egg cartons to follow you
through the aisles of burning fluorescents.
Together we wandered down the blinking brightness
like leftover birthday balloons, floating
in a dizzy mass, eating the bright thoughts of carrots,
the candy of image and moment, small movement of a woman's
red shoe, brushing a penny into the aisle.
But the book ends abruptly. And always too soon.
I touch the face of your latest edition,
and walk towards checkout wondering,
how you fit the entire world in a single haiku.
Where will I eventually lose my wallet full of the keys to time?
What Los Angeles will you leave in your wake,
with poets and madmen circulating
through a crowd of Virgins and Crones, Medusas with their living
harpoons, held over our heads,
all of us shouting in the supermarket, dreading our association with roses,
eating chicken frozen, as we stand, bagging our own groceries

as we whistle your name, turning our sorrow to song,
humming to each other as we wait to be transformed
by that long transformational line.

–with thanks to Allen Ginsberg and Jack Grapes

BLOOMSDAY

Lee McCarthy

Yes because it was Bloomsday and I couldn't go online at the house there's no internet there on account of my mother's so old she can barely use the remote control and if I wasn't there the blasted TV would be on every second of the day as loud as you please that's the way it is when they get old I guess just sit in front of the telly and get anesthetized by drivel and she says she can't stand Steve Harvey but there she is watching *Family Feud* the couch dented in from sitting so much in the same spot then the phone rang and I picked it up are you a solicitor no I'm asking support to help babies that haven't been born her voice all righteous white lady doing volunteer work nothing else to do with her time well you're barking up the wrong tree missy if mine were alive they'd be 40 by now is that why people have kids someone to take care of them in their old age and me childless taking care of my mom wondering who will take care of a little late for that and it was a good thing I left LA when I did couldn't have left at a better time me all agitated my knickers in a knot when he texted me do you date but it wasn't his fault I suppose I had it in for myself when I put my leg in the air way up high sitting on the couch like it was nothing well they all get easily provoked thinking with their one small head yes but then I remembered I had a pussy I'd be driving down PCH with damp knickers O my God I have a pussy then I'd be in the swimming pool and I'd get sticky again what's the matter with me was I telling him I want it yes well it's too late to rewind the tape so I went to Ralph's and got a chicken first time in five years I was thawing Jean Jean you're young and alive and whatever he said opened the floodgates and my pussy was dripping as I stood over the sink eating chicken with my bare hands.

SOUL FOOD

Miranda Heller

My cupboards were bare –
nothing but capers,
a bottle of soy sauce,
faded green lentils
and a can of pumpkin meat
I bought, once, when the dog had the runs.
So I went to Ralph's to get a chicken
and some broccoli rabe.
and a bloom of garlic.

I chose a yellow onion,
its coppery rice-paper dress
already in shreds,
sweet, pale flesh exposed,
there, in the wooden bin.
I pressed my thumb into a cantaloupe,
put a kumquat to my nose,
chose a bunch of rosemary, freshly misted –
I don't need much to make a meal that sticks to my guts.
It's feeding the soul that confounds me.

And, yes, I've tried okra and ribs.
And, yes, I've made cornbread from scratch,
smothered biscuits in gravy,
boiled crawfish and peeled them.
But my cupboard stays bare –
nothing in it but hope.
So I'm thinking, next time
I'll try a different approach –
maybe a chicken from Whole Foods?

FINDING FOWL

David J. Wilzig

December 10, 1859, Concord, Massachusetts, a freezing winter's day when the Rav Shlomo had planned to visit families at outlying Boston villages. My luck, my darling wife Rivka invited him to spend Shabbos, Friday through Saturday night, at our home. That's no less than four meals and I am not a rich man. I spend my time schlepping my wares, pots, pans, utensils and the like, across rutted winter roads, often deep in snow to small outposts around Boston. Sometimes I spend the night in my cart, under quilts without a proper place to sleep and my wife, Gd bless her, invited this big shot rabbi to our house.

It's Friday and wouldn't you know, my luck, Meyer, the only shochet I knew, the only kosher butcher business in nearby Sudbury was out of town performing a bris in Lincoln. Rivka gave me specific orders to buy two chickens from Meyer but that was not to be. No chicken for the Rabbi's Shabbos dinner? Unthinkable.

How to find two kosher chickens? Or find two chickens and perform ritual slaughter? What was I to do? What did I know? I am no bible scholar with a detailed understanding of the rules of kashrut. I do, however, travel with my prayer book which had instruction as follows:

1. "Thou shalt slaughter of thy flock, which the Lord hath given thee, as I have commanded thee, and thou shalt eat within thy gates, after all the desire of thy soul." (Deuteronomy 12:21).

Great except that I had no flock and the only kosher butcher store was closed.

2. "Shehitah must be done with a swift, smooth cut of a sharp knife whose blade is free of any dent or imperfection."

No problem there, I had many sharp knives for sale and a sharpening stone was attached to the cart.

3. "Shehitah entails severing the trachea and the esophagus without (a) hesitation while drawing the knife, (b) excessive pressure or chopping,

(c) burrowing the knife between the trachea and the esophagus or under the skin, (d) making the incision outside the specified area, or (e) lacerating or tearing the trachea or esophagus, which could result from an imperfect blade."

I had done this a few times before with chickens and felt comfortable in performing the physical act in accordance with ritual requirements.

4. "The lungs of the animal must be carefully examined for defects by one who is reliable and qualified."

Here, here was the problem. I had the skill to slaughter the animal but knew little of defective chicken lungs. Rivka would know what to look for but then I'd have to tell her that I left this till the last minute and I'd hear, "Yoshuah, will you never learn...?" which I have no patience for. It is cold, the sun will set in a few hours, it will be Shabbos and one cannot cook on Shabbos. I need two damn chickens. I will do it, I will perform ritual slaughter, but first I need to find those chickens and I cannot buy from the goyim - es passt nicht.

"What to do, what to do, what to do," I asked Gd and myself as I drove my cart homeward praying for an solution. Gd spoke in my ear. "Do you see that house?" he asked. "Which house?" I responded. "That one," and my head turned to the right as I passed a house owned by Ralph, a famous writer, the one who wrote

> "I see all human wits
> are measured but a few
> unmeasured still my Shakespeare sits
> lone as the blessed Jew"

I could see that his side yard and backyard were filled with chickens. I can ask to buy two of them and if he's not home, teaching at Harvard or with that Longfellow poet, I can leave him payment with a note, then I can stop at the lakeside park, perform the ritual slaughter and never have to tell Rivka that I WENT TO RALPH'S TO GET A CHICKEN and afterwards prayed that Mr. Emerson wouldn't mind.

NO DANCING IN THE KITCHEN

Marilyn Conrad

I was kind to myself for two days this week,
in touch with what I needed
for my body and my spirit,
listening to my inner voice,
not scanning for the needs of others,
not trying to get it right,
not trying to fit in,
not trying to look normal.
Then today,
after writing class,
after lunch with Alexandra,
after stopping at Trader Joe's
for ravioli and yogurt
and Ralphs to buy a chicken,
when I thought I was coming home
to an empty house,
for open space
to follow my own rhythms,
I pulled into the garage,
and there, on the right hand side,
was the white BMW convertible.
Damn! My husband Robert was still home.
There he was:
3:00 in the afternoon
at the computer
working on his opposition brief
in his green robe and slippers
gray/brown hair sticking up
like a mad scientist.

No time alone in the house for me,
no coming and going from the computer,
no nap in the bedroom,
no *Downton Abbey* in the den,
no talking on the phone in the living room,
no writing,

no music,
no dancing in the kitchen,
no feeling inside for what wanted to happen next,
no listening to see what I was hungry for,
no opening my heart.

Instead, I hid out in my study,
reading a mystery novel,
eating peanut butter granola bars,
drinking ginger tea laced with rum.

I don't know how to live
in front of other people –
not with my whole self –
not even with Robert.
I cover my mouth with my left hand
as I write those words
and return
to my pretend life.

THE BREATH AND THE WAVE

Lori Grapes

So I'm going to Ralph's to get a chicken and I remember that night, August 2nd, 1991, after we finished a movie we rented, the one where Julia Roberts fakes her own death to escape the husband who charms then dominates her, and my water breaks.

I rush into the shower to shave my legs while my husband rushes around the apartment on Orange, filling a bag with essentials. Then we get in the car and he insists on stopping at Ralph's for ice. Just like him, I think, to have made a list, to prepare for the future by writing it all down, the words like stones we walk on to get to the next place, the further shore, the country of blocks and sticks for swords.

But our son is in no rush to enter a world he hasn't imagined himself. It is just like him, we come to see. But that night on the way to the hospital, all I know is that he is in no hurry, and there is no pain. The ice? The ice is for Jack to cool my brow as I labor. I wait in the car as he runs in. He buys an ice chest too, a blue one made of styrofoam, and he stands in the parking lot pouring the cubes into the chest, the need for a cool head increasingly clear as we drive toward the hospital.

He is so precise, my husband. The contractions begin and it's time to breathe, in and out, as the wave comes and goes. But no, Jack says, it's important to get it right. How about the ice, I say. To cool my brow? But no, Jack says, we have to figure out this wave thing, this breathing thing that goes with the wave. Forget the wave, I say, get me some ice, or better yet, some pain medication. No, no, no, says Jack. The wave, the breath, the order is important. But the pain, I say. What about the pain and the ice and the baby who is ready now?

I think you breathe out, says Jack, as the wave recedes, the way you breathe out as you lift weights. That has to be it. When you think of it that way, it makes perfect sense. He takes the lid off the ice chest, finds a cube, and moves it across my forehead as he listens to my breath, louder now as I begin to push, and the dawn approaches, and the ice in his hand melts to become water, to become ocean.

FORGET ABOUT THE AXE

Linda Neal

I eat meat, always have,
except for that brief time in 2011
I did the vegan thing.
Most days I eat meat—
you know, a turkey sandwich,
barbequed ribs, a juicy lamb chop.

Some piece of an animal—
a leg, a breast, a wing, even a tongue,
of a lamb a pig, a steer, a bison, a chicken,
(not a sheep, a rooster, a milk cow or a buffalo).
I have my boundaries.
I've never eaten a boar.

I'd never dream of eating
a horse, a dog, or a cat cut up
in a garlicky sauce on my dinner plate.
Never a dolphin or a whale,
a blue-footed booby or a Galapagos penguin.

I make crazy distinctions,
leave some critters to roam the land,
dive their way through the water
or fly across the sky,
put others on my plate.
I don't eat their eyes or their noses
but I swear, trout cheeks are a sweet treat.

It's eat or be eaten, a kind of natural law,
but I wall myself off from the killing,
don't kill them myself, don't pull off
their skin or their feathers,
like my grandpa did, after he chased
a chicken around the yard with an axe.
I don't dig out lambs' hearts,
or chop up their livers for fun.

I just eat meat—fish too.

I forget about the gun, the axe,
the bow and arrow, the feed lot and guillotine.
I just say to hell with it all, and tell myself
"I think I'll go to Ralph's and get a chicken."

THE NUMBERED SQUARE

Renu Chopra

The usual drama. She said and then I said and then I thought about what I should have said and why she said what she did and then I didn't sleep all night but stayed under the covers and played Sudoku on my iPad in an effort to distract my brain enough to let it to allow me to get some sleep. I've moved myself up to the difficult level. I can't figure out how the hint function of the game is making such rash decisions. I know there must be logic to it but my brain is not a genius level brain and it takes it time to figure out simple things. Why must a 7 go into the 5th row? Why must it?

The next day I forget about it until lunch when in-between bites of my Jersey Mike California club sandwich, no bacon. I forgo reading *The Elegance of the Hedgehog* to have another go at the elegance of the numbered square. I'm still in confusion as to how the logic works so instead I go to Ralph's to get a chicken. I look for the organic label and can't find it, look for the depth in my day and can't find it, look in the rows and rows of canned food, fresh food, pasta, potato chips, protein drinks and kitchen items until I see that I don't know what I am looking for.

Not true. I know I am looking for the 5, for the 'must', for the understanding of the must, so that I can then rebel against it and shout it out, to the world out my window and out to the vacant vacuum air

"I am the blink of my mother's eyes, I am not her. I am the rebel of my ancestors, but I am not them. I am the space in between you and him, the pause between the whisper and the command, the fusion between the curry and the pasta, the stop of the implication of the gossip, the air in the connection of two friends talking, the longing of Thursday's class. I am the intersection of the row and the column. I am organic, I am not a 5, I am infinity!"

HAPPY BIRTHDAY, JACK

Lauren Levine

"Happy Birthday, Jack," she spoke into the dawn.

Her dress was a cheap, designer rip-off she'd spotted on the rack at her neighbor's yard sale. She was a pear squeezing into a dress made for an apple, but those that knew her would say she was much more of a peach. She thought it was because she was the sweetest thing around, but the truth was she had a rock hard center, and a lot of facial hair. She was, it turned out, a full fruit salad. You know the type. She sat on the swing, on her porch, with the loose board that needed fixing. A nail. Freed itself and sat smugly, by her chair. Each *to* made a cry, each *fro* made a yawn. The sun rose up over the Poplar trees, the evergreens haloed in this glorious, new day sun. She swung back and forth, thinking about the loose board that needed fixing, thinking about the chicken she needed to pick up at Ralph's, and watched. Best seat in the house. She knew how much he disliked people giving him birthday cake, so she decided to take the $1400.00 she'd raised and send it to him as a gift.

"Happy Birthday, Jack," she said to herself. "Have a very Happy Birthday."

BLAST YOU, JACK GRAPES!

Mari Weiss

SO   (pause)   do the exercise just do the...

    I   don't   know   what   to   **BLAST!**

my brain   **WENT** blanksouthrotteninthestateof

Shakespeare, YOU bastard

   pen   **TO**   paper   scribble

scribble JOT jot

     how many   **RALPHS**   does it take

       TO   write an Image Moment

well?   wait wait don't tell me   **SEVEN!**

Step Right Up   and **GET**   your $1400

     would you like that in Chex Mix

               or, perhaps,

      A rubber

                CHICKEN   ?

TIMING

Lisa Segal

I'd gone to Ralphs to get a chicken, but there I was in the wine aisle. Ganesh was over by the reds. You know Ganesh. The remover of obstacles? The patron of arts and sciences? The deva of intellect and wisdom? Well, anyway, he, too, seemed to be looking for a bottle of wine. As he looked, he juggled a squirt gun, an axe, an apple, and a water lily. A shopping basket with a plastic-wrapped chicken was in his third hand. His fourth was in the pocket of his sweat pants.

"Excuse me," I said, "aren't you Ganesh?" He didn't hear me over Hugh Laurie's "St. James Infirmary." A gold sequin glinted on the floor. A mouse nibbled a potato chip at his feet.

"Excuse me," I umbrella-ed, "you're Ganesh, aren't you?"

He stopped juggling. His skin was yellow, if from the florescent lights, or not, I couldn't tell. With his trunk, he swished off his reading glasses and cleared his throat.

"Yes," he said, "I am." His blue eyes sparkled, happy to be recognized. "Do you want to hear a duck joke?"

"Seriously?" I said. "A duck joke?"

"Yeah," he said, "Do you have five minutes? I got a million of 'em, but my favorite's the one about a duck who goes into a bar and asks the bartender if he's got any grapes. Have you heard that one?"

"The only duck joke I know," I said. "is the one my mom tells and it ain't about any duck going into a bar."

Ganesh bent down, grabbed the mouse by its tail, straightened up, and ambled over. The mouse, clutching its potato chip, dangled from one hand, the basket with the chicken from another. He held the items he'd been juggling against his belly. When he got to me, he set his basket down next to mine.

"What're you looking for?" he said.

"A dry white," I said.

"Try this one," he said. "It's got a way with words." He handed me a bottle of "Don Uve." The slogan 'Beloved of Believers Everywhere' ringed a drawing of a bunch of grapes. "But don't take any wooden nickels." His hand was out of his pocket. His fingers flicked next to my ear. "Take this instead." He showed me a coin.

"A buffalo nickel!" I said.

"Well," he said, "I see one doesn't have to get up that early to fool you."

"Hey," I said, "What do you think I am, dumb or— "

"TIMING!" he said. He laughed and dropped the nickel in with my radishes. "Don't forget there's a buffalo inside a circle doing the cha-cha-cha with your vegetables."

"I won't," I said.

"Also don't forget," he said, "that you never know what'll happen when you go to Ralphs to get a chicken."

"Now there's a true sentence," I said.

He gathered his basket and turned to walk away.

"Hey," I said, "what about the duck joke?"

Noises came from his basket. The wrapping around his chicken burst. Feathers sprouted from under the chicken's pale skin. A mallard's green head peeked above the edge of the basket and blinked at me. It preened its wings, quacked, and flew off over the baked goods.

"Next time," he said, "I'll tell you two of 'em next time."

I HAVE TO GO TO RALPH'S

Terry Stevenson

and get a chicken
I'd rather celebrate
the anniversary of the mapping
of the human genome
and the last concert Elvis ever gave,
but I have to buy a chicken.
Not just any chicken –
my chicken must be free range,
with no hormones or antibiotics,
fertile and ready to lay eggs.
My chicken is a hybrid,
inside it beats a human heart,
grown from my stem cells.
The heart is for me
so that I can finally feel love.
There's no love at Ralph's or in me.
I need this heart.
I need my chicken heart.

THE FLOGGINGS WILL CONTINUE

Elya Braden

After 11 days on Dr. Kellyann's starch-free, dairy-free, sugar-free, alcohol-free bone broth diet, I dream of spaghetti carbonara, the twirl of pasta on my fork, the bite of gluten between my teeth, the tang of garlic clawing the back of my throat. It returns me to Cent'Anni, that quaint trattoria in Greenwich Village where I celebrated the closing of a major acquisition with my clients, then threw up in my hotel room. Stomach flu. Or maybe the rumbling anxiety of working for a psycho law partner whose philosophy of associate management boiled down to "The floggings will continue until morale improves." After two weeks of subsisting on bagels, bananas and rice, I knew better but I didn't care. I was hungry and wanted to binge on pleasure—scarf down another doughnut, read another chapter of that trashy novel, kiss the girl, fuck the boy, slurp the pasta. The story of my life.

In my dream, I don't return to my hotel room. I wander the streets of Greenwich Village. It's nighttime and the moon hangs so full and round and low, I reach up and grab it. Pluck it from the sky and kiss that smiling white mug until the earth reverses on its axis, the tides flee from the shore, the man in the moon grows a body, arms and legs and skips away down the narrow sidewalk and into a jazz club while I float up into the heavens: incandescent, powerful, rock-hard, and ready to be worshipped from afar.

I wake up and it's Tuesday, day 12, and hurray! I've made it through another broth fast day. My skinny jeans are calling. Today I get to eat again. So I went to Ralphs to get a chicken.

SO I WENT TO RALPH'S TO BUY A CHICKEN

Chanel Brenner

On the way to my car, I stare

at the bougainvillea my husband gave me

seventeen years ago. It's flourishing

voluptuous fuchsia blooms.

For years it sat dormant,

not dead, but not blooming.

Why now? What has changed?

I drive past the preschool,

roll down my spotted window

and see children spread out

on the playground

like a strong wild garden

blowing in the wind.

I pass the pink van on Lincoln Boulevard,

"Topless Maids Wanted."

I envision breasts

ripe as pomegranates,

a feather duster resting

between mountains of spices.

When I return home,

 I discover a drip line

in the bougainvillea planter

our gardener must have installed.

I DRANK THE *JACQUES GRAPPA* AND REMEMBERED SQUAT

Bill Ratner

I was hungry. I was dirty. At least that's what my 8th grade chorus teacher Miss Dewey said about the way I wrapped my lips around the lyrics of "Onward Christian Soldiers." Love that frikkin' song. So I went to Ralphs to get a chicken, and they'd shuttered the goddamned place. Laid off dozens of union workers and put up a *365 By Whole Foods. What the fuque is that?* Yeah, it's open 365 but it sure ain't open 24/7, more like 10/6. I sauntered into this brand new concrete fluorescent icebox, as flat and colorless as Pat Boone's haircut in 1955, and I thought, where's the beef? Scratch 'em if you got 'em. Hungry? Hell, I need a drink. I didn't care if it was H2O, Jim Beam, or a coupla' oz. of tanker-ale they rail in from Bakersfield to keep Angelinos high.

Then I saw it on a shelf in the liquor section – a gleamy, dreamy, bottle-in-brown of *Jacques Grappa*, the type of swill you'd find in the desk drawer of a bad boss who bought it in Duty-Free before an Alaska Air flight from Portland. On the label was this Falstaffian type of guy who, if he stepped off the bottle, he would skate across the ice and steal a puck from a Russkie. Whispy whiskers, pinky face, a winky-wanky look about him. *Jacques Grappa*. Who would name themselves after a 90-proof Italian dessert wine made from used skins and pulp?

I paid the clerk, walked to my car, and I drank that bottle of *Jacques Grappa*. After that, I don't remember much except what my parole officer told me – I went on a tear, stealing coffee from 7-11, messing up the ladies' shoe racks in Nordstrom, and submitting a half-baked prose-poem to an online lit-mag I'd never even heard of named *Squat*. And then I waited – for the headache to go away, for the acceptance from *Squat* to arrive in my inbox, and for my memory to clear so I could see that face again – *Jacques Grappa*.

Who is this guy? Is he the winged muse-in-silk on the bottle of Canadian fizz-water? Is he that bearded ramp model selling Arrow shirts in display ads in *Playboy Magazine*? Is he the fellah Norman Rockwell drew as Santa Claus, having downed a few too many in a ranchero bar on Western south of Pico?

I remember *Jacques'* eyes – not so much beady, as ready. I'd say eagle-eyed, but I really mean pigeon-toed. And on that bottle of *Jacques Grappa* he's dressed in sneakers, sweats, and a pre-owned golf shirt that make him look like he's up on charges for illegal electronic surveillance.

Six months later *Squat.com* emailed me: *Thanks for your submission. Your words took the air out of the room.*

Would I drink a bottle of *Jacques Grappa* again? You bet your bippie I would. What the hell do I care about brain cells. I got a million of 'em.

I love you, *Jacques*.

EAT

Alexis Rhone Fancher

Your open 'fridge is the floodlight at a Hollywood premiere, a beacon for gourmands, a newly-minted saint. It lights up Sunset Blvd. from Olivera Street to the beach. Your smile is the blancmange of my sugar crave. It bowls me over, makes me gluttonous, ravenous, makes me eat gelato, and pomme frites, lick pasta with prosciutto in red sauce from the hollow of your throat, makes me want to eat pussy, and cheesecake, and macaroons, wash it all down with a robust Amorone, tamp it down with unfiltered, brown, Sherman cigarettes, makes me want to eat my way down your menu. So I went to Ralph's to get a chicken, cooked it just the way you like it, with mushrooms and onions and truffle oil, stuffed it with wild rice and naked photos of Ursula Andress, served it in the kitchen of my high-rise on Spring Street, watched you eat it, wolf it down, the same way I'd like to eat you.

4 HAIKU 4 U 2

Mia Sara

So, I went to Ralph's
(disguised as a birthday cake)
to get a chicken.

Many times I've thought,
what's with all this Ralph's chicken?
What about the cake?

But Jack Grapes taught me
the magic of Ralph's chicken,
and he's no dumb cluck.

He's a birthday boy,
counting his chickens before
hatching his poets.

MIDNIGHT AT RALPHS

Lois Nightingale

I went to Ralphs and got a chicken. I didn't stay long. I marched out so no
one would notice me.
Exit stage left,
your mother was home when you left,

you're right,

your father was home when you left,

you're right,

your sister was home when you left,

you're right,

sound off,
one, two,
sound off,
three four,
bring it on down,
one, two-oo
three four.
sound off,
breaking down,
the surface of
the world stage,
you're left—

Gisella recognized me, "Yo Doc, t'ain't Tofurkey. That's the real deal
there." She spun an empty receipt spool and squinted at me through cat-
eye glasses, missing a couple rhinestones.

They dim the overhead store lights for restocking. One sliding glass door
is barricaded after midnight. I forget which one. The red-head works the
night shift. Her name badge hangs from a checkered lanyard. There's a
discount barcode on the back of it, 50% off Soyrizo and 30% off my Fakin'
Bacon. "Lucky finds," she always says and whistles a Doppler. Lucky's her
rescued Chihuahua-mix.

Tonight her stare said, *"Curly B-12-deprived celery-crunching shrink
pretend she can goose-step that free-range into some bad seitan."*

My reusable bag at the end of the conveyor belt twirled in time to
the Muzak.   31

"Uh," I said. "I um, had to go to Ralphs to buy a chicken."

She flicked the plastic roll into the trash. "And what are *you* gonna do with it?" she asked. She was spanging for Lucky.

"The time has come," I cleared my throat, "for every fowl murderer to face justice. For we know not the day nor the hour, nor if the chicken came before the egg, but let there be no doubt that this cold-blooded butchered hen, blinded by beheading and plucked bare—even's got a naked eye," I pointed to the hole between its shoulders, "was once some poor brooding mother's chick. Some life, no?"

"Of all the sad angels Doc, get ahold of yourself!" Gisella said, "Just pretend there's a time to sing, a time to dance and a time to buy yourself a fucking chicken."

An over-cologned bag boy smacked my Ralph's ecofriendly bag against the stainless steel. It opened.
I stepped into his personal space and bounced the chicken in front of his pock-marked smug mug. "Then it'll dance. See, see, and the running form, naked, Blake, right Blake? it's naked, naked as a jaybird! Except it's a goddamned bald chicken!"

Blake, the special-needs FLSA worker who's paid pennies under Ralph's special wage certificate, stretched out the stubby wings of my cold dead sentient. He bowed toward its invisible head and stuttered, "Per-perchance, in all your tr-travels have you ever been to Pi-pittsburgh?"

"Oh for chrissake," I said.

Blake's laminated nametag swung as he made my headless chicken dance. "Justice by Savage Peace" played over the sound system, we all sang along.

A sticker with number six kept reappearing on the conveyor belt. Seven is a frozen number.

All Ralphs' chickens Jack, have *fresh* moves.

LE DÉJEUNER SUR L'HERBE

Dana Berman Duff

A bear lumbered up from the hollow.
He had a small boy in his jaws.
I was eating a drumstick.
We had planned a picnic in the wild,
so I went to Ralph's to get a chicken
and now, on a blanket we'd unfolded over the
duff, in a clearing between the trees, soft
with pine needles that afforded a place to rest
and restore our strength with food, we'd taken a
luncheon break in our mountain hike.
We looked at the bear and he paused. We paused.
Flies buzzed in the filtered sunlight, attracted to the meat.
The boy didn't move at all so I supposed he
was dead. Too late—there was
no one to save and nothing to do.
We sat still. The bear stood still.
Eventually, the bear turned and moved
into the gloom of the great forest
and was lost to our sight.
We resumed eating, the bear with his lunch
and we with ours.

CONNECTING THE DOTS

Shira Fox

So I went to Ralph's to get a chicken and on my hungry way, I began to trickle a thought-form of the truthful sort – that is – Jack Grapes makes my gauntlet giggle.

The night skies rise up to meet me when I'm riding his salt and pepper coattails. It's a lovely bit of business really... all rubbed against my talent and my genius in spiritual war fare for the ages; how do you like them apples; he ripens my talent; makes me robust with trust I've something to offer & that makes my smile ready to fall off the tree. Getting to study with him is like sunshine oozing out of a toothpaste tube, but one that's endless, streamed forth from infinity.

He's a silly goose with a Ph.D. in the best of words and the human soul and the place these dance together. A swordsman for the creative heart, ready to cut out the tongues of the naysayers in my mind, ready to help me bleed them out, right onto the paper, where they'll pay me back, showering light, like stars I've no idea how I placed in the sky, & yet they hang... singing "Ode to Jack Grapes, my teacher, my knight."

BLACK AND BLUE AND PURPLE

Vanessa Poster

Jack, my writing teacher, said,
"Come walk with me around the block."

This was during my first marriage, the bad one.

The jacaranda purple puddles filled the street.
One lone blossom lay squished on the sidewalk.
It was a short shirtsleeves sort of day.
His a blue button-down, mine a black t-shirt.

I love walking through the dapple of light from blossomed branches.
I love the movement and the freedom and the dance.

"You know," Jack said, "a marriage does not have to be filled with yelling."

My heel stuck in a crack and I splattered right there all purple and dappled.

So that night, I went to Ralph's to get a chicken.

Two years later, I got a divorce.

FOOT DOWN BEAK SNAP IN BULLOCK COUNTY ALABAMA

Jan McGuire

The minute I stepped foot in the grass I'd mowed yesterday there under the Jackson's clothesline my legs, practically up to my knees, got covered in fleas. I don't think I'd ever seen them that bad this early on so I called first to make sure he was still home then jumped back in the truck, tore outta there and went to Ralph's to get a chicken. His place is only a couple miles down Pettus Road from mine, and by the time I got there (pretty much like he always does) he'd come up with an even better idea and that was to lend me a couple of his guinea hens. He swore they'd out smart chickens any day for gobbling up fleas and told me about the time he'd seen one hop up at least ten or twelve feet and snap a yellow jacket outta thin air right before it was about to go for old man Richter's head when he was painting the siding on his shed last fall.

It all started when old man Richter took something Ralph had said the wrong way, got heated up and mumbled some nasty retort under his breath but when Ralph shot back, "What'd you say to me?" old man Richter, without taking his eyes off that brush and without missing a stroke, said, "I'm talking to the paint." Then before Ralph even had a chance to open his mouth next thing you hear is the snap of that guinea hen's beak.

Just snap, snap and snap! Kindly like some kinda weird metaphoric sequence of events or something if you know what I mean.

DRUMSTICK

Merry Elkins

I went to Ralph's to buy a chicken. There was one left on the heat shelf and it was this chicken without a leg. I reached for it, then drew my hand back. Who would buy a one-legged chicken?

Then I found myself feeling sorry for the chicken and wondered what happened to the poor thing and if it was born like that or lost its drumstick in a crash landing trying to fly or in a fight with another chicken.

I got to thinking about the man in the wheelchair in the Marine Corps T-shirt I saw on the trail underneath the Hollywood Sign yesterday, the right leg of his beige shorts sewn together, covering what was left of his thigh, his eyes focused upward towards the Sign, like he was looking to God for an explanation.

How is it there's just a nanosecond between being a hot-shit-young GI in a bar looking to score with the girl sidling up to you and being on a military hospital cot, looking down at the empty space that was once your leg? How is it there's such a fine filament between life and death, youth and old age, humor and tragedy? How is it?

How do you mend after that, knowing it's impossible to be the same as you once were, to walk the same as you did, smile as you did, laugh as you did, think as you did? Your soul plundered by circumstances, your life robbed by fate, your heart buried in rubble, when you were once, Rome.

One minute my mother was standing in a gas station waving goodbye to me after I'd left her off to pick up her car. "I love you," I'd said and hugged her before I got back into my car to leave. She was thin, frail. I felt like I was hugging a piece of glass that would crack if I hugged too hard. I always see her in a green suit when I play that moment back in my head. Or maybe it was that her car was green. A racing green Chrysler Imperial with dark green leather seats. She loved that car. We called it the moving living room. The next time I saw her, she was in a hospital bed plugged in to a breathing machine with her eyes taped shut, the red polish rubbed off
her fingernails.

I'm older now than my mother was when she died. I see wrinkles in the mirror that she never got to see on herself. The aches in my back and hip tell me I'm getting up there, yet I'm still trying to figure it all out, to get it right, to make it mean something, to take it all in.

I grabbed the chicken, took it up to the checkout and stood in line. When my turn came, I put the chicken down in front of the woman at the register. She was wearing a nametag that said, "Ruth" pinned on a T-shirt that had Siamese cats all over it. I may have imagined it, but she gave me a look that said, "Why are you buying a chicken with one-leg?" But she said nothing. She just rang me up, put the chicken in a brown Ralph's bag, then looked at the next person in line. That was it. She didn't give me another thought. In a nanosecond, I was just a memory.

THE GRAND RENAISSANCE HOTEL

Suzanne O'Connell

It's one of those swanky joints.
The bellhop greets me in his silk vest,
with a round pillbox hat strapped under his chin.
"Bonsoir Monsieur," he says.
"Knock it off pal, which way to le elevatoire?"
He gives me a curse-eye but says nothing,
pointing to the rear wall.

I am going to the pool on the roof.
City view up there, free cocktails,
starlets in bikinis and all that crap.
Not my type of crowd.
I'm here on business not pleasure.
I've been told a woman is having trouble
with her thug of a husband.
I'm supposed to talk some sense into him.
He gets jealous and forgets she's not a rug
he's trying to beat the dust out of.

The elevator is self-service.
I slide the accordion door shut
and push the mahogany button--
R for roof. The walls are covered
with golden curlicues and googaws.
I feel underdressed but at least
I remembered to remove my hat.

The door opens to a warm summer night.
The starlets are gone,
maybe dressing for dinner.
No thugs either.
It's dark except for the lights under the water.
The whole city sparkles, making the job worth it.
The pool is a blue jewel on black velvet.
Piped in guitar music plays a love song.

A woman floats face down on the water.
Her hair is spread out like seaweed,
her white dress a transparent jellyfish.
I was sent here on business.
Looks like I'm too late.
I wish I'd gone to Ralph's for a chicken
instead of coming here!

BEFORE IT'S TOO LATE

Cirelle Raphalian

Champagne is being poured with no concern for money or time of day. Eleven-thirty a.m. must seem like a good time to start celebrating. The slur of words followed by phony laughter cast a shadow of distrust over the party guests gathered around the poolside bar.

I knew it was a mistake to accept the invitation. I came for Helena, not her fiancé Bradley, who is working the crowd. "Treacherous bastard," I mumble. I glance around in hope no one heard me. A couple of cool customers nearby give me a sideways glance.

Just then a long-fingered hand with scarlet painted nails, the color of roses on a lover's casket, and a five carat rock, pushes open the sliding glass door. Helena steps out like she's on the promenade deck of the QE2. High heeled gold sandals on her well-manicured feet, sun browned arms and legs and a trim body with all the right stuff in all the right places. A translucent kaftan, the color of a desert sunrise, floats around her. A pair of gold-framed sunglasses in her right hand, a glass of champagne in her left. Every head turns in her direction. The fragrance of Tahitian gardenia precedes her. She puts on her sunglasses with a gesture that could send a country to war. I take a sip of champagne. I wish I hadn't given up smoking. Why had I given it up smoking?

Helena smiles and waves at the party guests like some kind of goddamn European royalty. She knows how to pull off an entrance. The gal has a PhD in class. And the cash to back it up. She is a catch, and the bastard had cast his line and caught her hook, line and sinker.

I hear her laugh as she walks in my direction. I wish to escape this awkward meeting, but how? I know I'm a hypocrite, I know to the depth of my bones. I know I cannot not face Helena and not implore her to reconsider her rash, romantic, race to the alter. I know there must be some explanation why she is doing this. Trepidation hangs on me like a sweaty linen suit.

If I don't tell her soon that I'm in love with her it will be too late. I'll lose her to that bum.

A dull bang like the backfire of a truck splinters the air. A woman screams. I turn to see Bradley fall to the flagstone. Blood stains his immaculate white jacket.

Yesterday in desperation I called Helena's best friend.

"I'm sinking like a stone," I said.

She laughed, but she didn't like the slime bag anymore than I did.

"You are a sap." she chided me.

"I know, a miserable sap. I wouldn't trust the guy to go out to Ralph's to buy a chicken."

"Shall we hatch a plan?" she said.

"I like the way you're thinking. Do you have something in mind?"

"Let me give it some thought," she replied and lit a cigarette.

Damn, why did I stop smoking?

THE GAME OF FUCK, MARRY OR KILL

Megan Wolpert Dobkin

Let's bury it together.
We can say we never saw a thing—
my banded trigger finger
my chipped scarlet nail
pull back my thumb hammer
turning point to our fairy tale.

Wink. Wink.
It's gone now.
Isn't it?
Miraculous.
I don't hear a thing.
Not a peep. Not a moan.

Nothing to remind me
of the times I went to Ralph's
to buy a chicken,
but all I found were bones.
We promise each other,
we do solemnly swear
not to fall to our regrets
in this, our parlor game.
So, which is it then? Fuck, marry or kill?
And what's the counterclaim?
Oh dear.
Just…take your hand in mine.
Let's put our shovels aside
and have ourselves some nice cold tea
and silently count the verbs
we all along could of had.
But, who's to say?
Come on. Let's face it,
two out of three ain't bad.

RADIO MAN

Jessica Pappas

I used to have fantasies of mingling with the rich and famous, maybe a good dose of celebrity elbow rubbing would be what I needed to feel like I matter. Would the special ones recognize me as one of them, special? Would they see me like I so craved to be seen? These are things I thought about while I was holed up on my corduroy couch recovering from Stan. I made no effort to care for myself I turned down every invitation, hid myself away, this was gonna take a while.

Then my friend Christine called me from New York and told me she had to find a date for a friend of a friend of a friend to go to the premier of *Oceans 11* and would I mind. This must be my reward for the pain and suffering of the past eleven years, I don't mind. "He is kind of a big deal," she said, "His name is Radio Man, he wears a radio around his neck he's homeless but famous homeless." And she hung up. Red-carpet after-party the whole nine yards, she must not mean homeless, homeless. All that mattered was I was about to be on the arm of someone important and that will make me important.

I was standing in a mosh-pit of photographers, watching as each limo pulled up and someone famous got out. Fans gated off to the side, screaming as one celebrity after the other smiled graciously for cameras. My heart was pounding with anticipation. A surge of grandiosity lifted my spine I was flying, I'm no longer on the outside looking in finally, I matter. I am too-cool-for-school.

The next limo door opened and with it a stench that made me time-travel to places I never wanted to go. There he was, my date recognizable by the old-fashioned radio hanging around his neck over his disheveled suit, his greasy hair grown into his nappy beard. "Jessica," he gargled almost choking on years-old saliva stuck in the crevices of his mouth. A shiny penny on the ground squashed by his tattered shoe before I could make a wish, a wish this wasn't my date. I was frozen in limbo between dreams and delusion's. I could feel the helium of my inflated ego seeping through the fragile cracks of my soul. The truth of myself flashed before me in the lights of Paparazzi, I'm nothing and my date is homeless. He's standing in front of me I'm trapped. "ChristinesaidyouprettyyouareIdontdrink?" he mumbled and followed with blowing his nose in his hand.

I have to get back to my couch. I have to get a rabies shot.I have to kill Christine.

He moved in closer."Igottapeemeetyouinsidek?" A ball of spit landed on my cheek. NO IT'S NOT OK. "I'm sorry I just remembered I have to go to Ralph's and buy a Chicken, rain-check?" I didn't wait for the answer.

I DIDN'T CHICKEN OUT

Bambi Here

Jack was in the kitchen
baking a vegetarian quiche
—not what I expected
but I had gone to Ralph's
to get a chicken
cuz he told me to . . .
god knows why
and since he was kind
he licked my drumsticks

squinting like a drunk
in the 8 am sunlight
from last night's stupor
I listened to him listen
to my baby steps

my chest opened
tear drops spilled
out of my underground
cornered between heaven
and a well of mediocrity
I waited for the wind
(and the open window)
to cool my thickness

if it wasn't for his students
in colorful words
if it wasn't for his squirt gun
chasing me into the back yard
if it wasn't for his embrace
rippling into my memory

I would not have seen
him look at me—
really look at me
there in that kitchen

in horrid overhead light
yet—
I was seen for the first
time
ever
on October 6th, 2010

ONE STOP ON THE WAY TO LAX

Baz Here

went to Ralph's to get a chicken
on Sunset just west of La Brea
age 23
walked home to Martel just above Fountain
east of Vista

I was a pop song lost
and a bullet of judgment
Turned inward
negative $567
an army of overdraft fees
and a closet of fingernails biting

walking down Fuller
to grab a bag of chips at Trader Joes
I tripped on a nail and
fell into my childhood

the taste of Play Doh in my mouth
and the smell of roasted potatoes
from the kitchen, Mom telling Dad
"your son was so cute today, singing into his tape recorder,
y'know, he can really carry a tune."
Dad frowning, "Please God, don't let him be an artist."

I lie on the sidewalk, blood on my knees
failure in my gut
a plane ticket in my pocket.
it's time to go home
I called a cab

somewhere on the way to LAX
Wilshire and Sweetzer to be exact
there was a man
sitting in his sweatpants
armed with a squirt gun

and a fart machine
burying people's agonies
and he looked at me
straight through my childhood
grabbed the plane ticket in my hand
crumbled it up
stuck it in his mouth
and with one swallow

saved my life

FOLLOWER

Niksa Smith

My name is Niksa Smith and I'm the most interesting person that I know. I'm not joking… I also love myself too much and usually I don't care what you think. If you ever ask me if we are on the same page I will say "yes" but in the reality we aren't even reading the same book. I was a kid when life (and death) taught me how to be a leader. Leader of my own life. But there is a trick, in order to be a successful leader you have to be a good follower, you have to be a selective follower, willing to question yourself, rebuild, learn, steal, evolve, grow, die and born all over again.

I have a tattoo that says "Destroy my desires; eradicate my ideals, show me something better and I will follow you". It's a quote by Dostoyevsky, I did follow him, as well as Machiavelli, Mandela, all of the victims that my country killed – name by name so they never forget them, black people against me and my white privilege, my broken heart – several times, I did follow vodka for a while too. Was it easy? Not at all, it was hard, it was always the road less traveled, lonely, painful and a long walk to freedom. But it was worth it! Every fucking each time. They are all still behind that quote and that's exactly what makes me the most interesting to myself, that everlasting journey, that journey that is pushing me to live, not to exist.

During that journey to unknown, because destination isn't important, I followed one more person, I followed him to Ralphs to get a chicken. It was a challenge to be a follower again, but when I got back home, I got back as a writer.

Thank you Jack, for allowing me to follow you.

THE WRATH OF GRAPES

Bev Feldman

In spite of honking Fiats below them, twenty-one monk-hooded black and white Capuchin pigeons strut, bow, twirl and fuck with avian abandon on the ancient stone window ledges. The setting Italian sun streams through old stained glass windows behind the ledges and illuminates a magnificent walnut-paneled red-velvet draped room from history. His Holiness the Pope, seated inside this room at his 15th century desk, assesses the situation in front of him: "Oh boy, I'm-ah gonna lose-ah the game, the game I NEVER lose-ah," he thinks (in Italian).

Jack Grapes, seated on the other side of His Holiness's desk in an uncomfortable 12th century chair long used for torturing pagans, launches his final move and says (also in Italian) "La vittoria e mio, your Holiness!" and jumps his King over the Pope's last four checkers. Game over.

"I'm a loosa- **checkers** to YACK GRAPES!" the Pope yells as he double-fist-pumps. "YACK Grapes, famoso poet and actor on the Stage of LIFE! YACK Grapes, no-adverbs guy!" he yells. Excitedly ($5). "Now I worship-ah **two** Jews… Jesus Christ and YACK Grapes!" The Holy Father picks up a beautiful white church linen woven, embroidered, starched and ironed by resentful feminist nuns, dabs his eyes, blows his nose, and tosses the wadded hanky onto his desk. Jack is lost in gazing over His Holiness's shoulder at the fucking pigeons on the ledge who are inspiring his next poem about going to the post office. The Pope's lips quiver. "YACK Grapes, is big big honor to ah-lose-ah to legend guy like-a YOU!! Mama Mia!"

Jack Grapes made peace with unbridled adoration decades ago, having recognized that there are certain responsibilities that a legend's just got to get handled at the beginning.

His Holiness clears his throat and snaps his fingers, and a Swiss Guard steps out from behind the red velvet curtain to Jack's right. The Pope signals the guard with a wag of his thumb in Jack's direction. The guard unholsters his weapon and hands it to Jack, handle first. "You-ah know-ah what to do, YACK," the Pope says. Jack laughs, takes the squirt gun and shoots the Pope in the face three times. Jack sets the squirt gun down on the table and says to His Eminence, "Please, your Holiness, use my hanky." Jack reaches into his sweatpants and offers His Holiness his treasured black Bukowski hanky. The Pope takes the sacred hanky and mops up the Holy Water on his face. "Grazi, grazi, Yack Grapes," the Pope says.

The heavy pagan torture chair makes a loud groan when Jack scoots it back and stands up. Twenty of the twenty-one fucking pigeons lift off the ledge and fly into the sunset on honeymoons. "Your Worship," Jack says to the Pope, "dinner's on me! I'm going to Ralph's to get a chicken." In Vatican Square there is a loud chorus of honking Fiats.

RED LAMPS

Jennifer Rose

I went to Ralph's the other day
to buy a chicken.
I walked to the aisle that holds the dead birds
soaking in their tin foil coffins,
suffocating, covered in Saran Wrap
bathing in their blood,
barely staying warm under the red lamps
in the display case,
waiting to be somebody's dinner.
It was just then I remembered—
I've been a vegetarian for 26 years.
I exited the market full of legalized murder,
said a small prayer for the dead birds
soaking in their tin foil coffins,
suffocating, covered in Saran Wrap
bathing in their blood,
barely staying warm under the red lamps
in the display case,
waiting to be somebody's dinner.

MY JACK

Brynn Thayer

I'd like to Write Like I Talk when I tell you how happy I am that you were born but that's very personal and I would probably have to use my Deep Voice.

If you want to know the dirty truth, I'd like to have a very Straight Talk with you about what you mean to me. So, here goes...

You weave magic with your Teeth and Mouth every Thursday night from 2-6.

My Mini Dice start to flutter when you walk through the door of 6535 and we won't even begin to discuss what happens to my Big Dice.

You are unreal and Surreal[ism] and the real deal and I go all Wild, Dark and Passionate when I see you smile.

All my Muses agree that you are the cat's pajamas and therefore, you should be Read and Sung everyday of your life.

Point me to your Lost World, Jack and I will follow you into the Field of Absence.

In your classroom, my Dreaded Ass[ociation] sits in the rocker to your right and lingers on your Image for a Moment too long.

As I Massage my Transformation Line, it's just too, too much to bear.

How shall I calm my frenzied soul?

I think I'll go to Ralph's and get a chicken.

Nothing else will squelch this mighty hunger.

I love you, Jack Grapes—
Happy Birthday.

FRANKIE THE 'FRAIDY CAT

Stuart Berton

Early in my life fear was a constant companion. I don't know why, but I just knew it existed. Whenever I would come out of our house I'd look to my left and then to my right, without ever moving my head. Then if all was clear on the perimeters I'd look straight ahead, then look left and right again. If there was no movement to be seen I would come out from under the doorway and purposefully follow my reason for coming outside. Even when I was with one or both parents I would do this. It took a while for them to catch on as to what I was doing, but they both thought it was a good thing for me to be aware of my surroundings, so they didn't give me any trouble when I continued to do it, even into my teens.

At school, too, I was easily spooked. On the playground I was always checking to see who was at either side of me or behind me. I liked to lean against walls because then I had no fear of someone sneaking up on me from behind. But with trees or benches I had no such protection, so I was constantly looking around if I were leaning against a tree or sitting on a bench.

My fear was so great that it overcame all the teasing directed at me. "Frankie, the 'Fraidy Cat" was what my schoolmates called me, ever since kindergarten, and that nickname stuck with me through grammar school and high school. When I graduated from high school my parents thought I should try living on my own, outside the parental umbrella, and they suggested that I find an apartment near a junior college on the other side of town and go to school there. They'd pay my expenses, and if I wanted to come home any time I could.

So I found an apartment there, and at the junior college no one in the student body knew me or even noticed me. I found I liked that kind of isolation, but I still was constantly on the lookout for someone who might do me harm, but no one seemed to notice me or care.

After a couple of months of classes, I became aware of this very pretty girl with long blonde hair who was in my English 101 class who kept looking at me and smiling. She was starting to creep me out. I didn't know why she would do that, and every time I looked back at her she'd wink at me. I really didn't know what to think or what to make of her behavior. Then one day she came out of class right behind me and tapped me on the shoulder as I went through the door. I turned around, fear in my eyes because I didn't know it was her. She said wanted to talk to me about something and suggested we go to the student union for coffee.

When we got in line to order she said, "I want to talk to you because I'm really curious. I don't ever see you hanging out with anyone, and I know you must miss that contact, so if you want someone to hang out with, I'm here. And if you want, I can introduce you to some of my friends, and then maybe they'll be your friends, too, and you won't have to be alone all the time. That alone stuff, it's not right. It can make people really creepy and dangerous and a little coocoo, and no one wants that. Hey, tomorrow night we're going to do a pot luck dinner at my apartment, and I'd like it if you could come. You can bring some barbecued chicken from the Ralphs that's just a couple of blocks from my apartment. Everyone would like that."

So I went to Ralphs and got a chicken. At the party I met her friends, six of them, three boys and three girls, and somehow, without exception, they were all actually pretty nice. And they listened when I talked. As we started preparing the meal and working together in the kitchen I got this weird feeling that these people actually liked me and enjoyed being with me. And I enjoyed being with them. I had never been in a situation like that with anyone other than my parents, and I found myself talking and being friendly and not looking around out of fear like I would usually do.

"Your nickname should be 'Smiley,'" one of the boys said, "because you're always smiling." I actually laughed when he said that. And then one of the girls said, "Smiley. That's cute, and it fits you." I have to say, I have never had a better time anywhere doing anything as I had that night. I was now no longer "Frankie, the 'Fraidy Cat." I was "Smiley" and it felt really good.

At the end of the evening, when everyone was saying their goodbyes, the girl from my English 101 class asked if I wanted to stay a little longer, maybe have a "nightcap". I was having such a good time I'd do anything, especially when she was the one who suggested it.

The "nightcap" turned out to be port, and it was the first time I'd ever had that to drink (or even heard of it, for that matter). She told me what it was and asked if I were game to try it. For her, I'd do almost anything, and so I did. It made me feel pretty good and pretty loosey-goosey, so when she kissed me I got into it like I've never gotten into anything before. Of course, nothing I had ever done before felt as good as I was feeling with her.

She knew I'd never had port before, and I think she knew I'd never had a romantic entanglement like I was having with her ever before.

When we were kissing I wanted to kiss her hard and soft and every which way and when her tongue touched mine I was totally in heaven. It felt soooo good.

Then she started to unbutton my shirt, so I thought I should unbutton hers, and when I started to do that she just smiled, and then gave me the biggest, hardest kiss anyone ever gave anyone else, probably in the history of the world.

And then she stood up, offered me her hand, which I took and then walked with her toward her bedroom. I had such a hard-on like I'd never ever dreamed possible. And that night was the best night of my life. I had totally new experiences I'd never had before and lost the virginity I really didn't want anyway. And when we woke up in the morning, after a long night of love-making and sleeping I was totally happy, happier than I could ever have dreamed.

Tomorrow night we're celebrating our tenth anniversary with our five-year-old son and our three-year-old daughter and our parents and our friends. Smiley and his wonderful, marvelous, miraculous, and generous sweet wife. Lucky, lucky, lucky me!!!

JACK, LOVE DAISY

Daisy McCrackin

Lori's cookin' is finger lickin'.
So I went to Ralph's to buy her a chicken,
But I took the Slausen Cutoff—oops!
All them chickens had flown their coops!
When at last the party I did make
Nothing there was left but cake.
"Happy Birthday, Jack," it said.
That just done-in my poor ol' head.
The "H", the "B", and the "J" I ate
And left the thing unfrosted!

CAT & CHICKEN

Arva Rose

It was raining. Hard. I was crouching forward like one of the witches in *Macbeth* trying to see what was going on through the one un-fogged spot on my windshield, when all of a sudden, this big black thing womp-smacked onto my hood. I couldn't tell what it was, I thought maybe a crow but then I could see it was holding on to the hood of the car right up near the front window, and god almighty…it was a cat. A cat! I am a cat person. I put on my flashers and managed to get to the curb. I got out and the cat, wet, frightened hanging on for dear life…was watching my windshield wipers go back and forth. I managed to pry her paws off the edge of the hood, put her in my coat and get back in the car. Cars still honking like crazy. I understood. I'd honk too. That's the problem with cars, we can't flip up a sign that says, my mother just died, or thank you! Or a cat just flung itself onto my car.

Cats don't like to be restrained. So the cat, a clawed animal was ripping my hands to shreds. I had to let go. And now had a wild meowling creature in the car. I had to get to Ralph's to buy a chicken. Originally, it was going to be a chicken I cooked. But I was an hour late and there had been these new developments, so now I was thinking more along the lines of rotisserie chicken. Then, a car rear ended me

It was a huge RANGE ROVER. A huge GOLD RANGE ROVER. That was more frightening than a flung cat. This petite blonde Stepford wife got out, T-shirt clinging like Bo Derek in 1987. She probably didn't have a dent on her fashion tank and I knew my poor little Ford was all crunched up in the back….and. OMG OMG I didn't hear a peep from the cat! I tried to look into the back but the cop and Bo were waiting for me. So, I got out…Bo and I exchanged info, then I found a space. I made sure the cat was all right. I locked the car and ran inside Ralph's. It was freezing in there, stuffed with people and more plastic cuidado signs than I knew existed. The lines were long.

I swooped a bunch of different cat foods into my carriage not knowing what flung cats ate. And I got the last sorry looking rotisserie chicken and some salad.

Now, my husband has a one-cat rule. We are a serially monogamous cat family.

But I was dying to know what the story was with this cat and already couldn't imagine ever giving him or her up.

I went to the pet shop next door a (surprising it is not IN Ralphs, alongside the pharmacy, the bank, and the coffee shop) and I bought a cheap cardboard carrier. I called my husband, and told him what happened. He was very sweet, considering how hungry I knew he was. I did say, since the chicken was already cooked, it wouldn't take much time to throw dinner together. Which is good, although he doesn't like rotisserie chicken, which is bad; and he did remind me of the one cat rule. As I was pulling out of the parking lot, I realized I didn't have my food. Or my purse for that matter. The cop stopped me and helped me get the wet bags of food off the roof and into my car, My purse, he didn't know from. I pulled over again. The cat still yowling, my hands still bleeding and spied it. On the ground. I had driven over it. My new purse, with my new wallet and new glasses. All shmushed.

But I did have my chicken.

AT RALPH'S BUYING A CHICKEN

Sherri Holzer

Summer in Los Angeles
Heat rising
Canopy of flames
Lean bodies burn poolside
Coconut and limes and seaweed

Kardashian lookalikes surround my cave
Those giant clam lips
Bleached strands of tentacles
Transgendered sharks take a bite
There is a confusing black hole in Calabasas Lake

Paparazzi on every corner
Bulbs flash while glaring eyes peek
It's not a mystery
Just a fact
Summer in LA at Ralphs buying a chicken

WHOLESOME

Liz Tynes Netto

Round and decent like an egg that longs
to be cracked
I walled in with unbreakable yearning,
envious
of the blasted bad who could become
great.
My measly transgressions not the stuff
for heroic
transformations, or saintly redemption.
A knife just for chopping,
a match
for lighting the grill. Finally maybe
it's okay now
that I go to Ralph's to get a chicken,
roast it
how I like it,
feed friends,
and later,
make a broth
with a pinch of salt
and the bones.

PRETTY IN PINK

Susan Benedict

Yesterday I went to Ralphs. I got a chicken. Something caught my eye in the parking lot. It was a check. On the ground. Right outside my car door. I picked it up, put it in the passenger's seat and ran errands. When I got home and looked at it, it was a cancelled check, not mine. From a Mr. Sherman in Pacific Palisades. For $200.00. From City National in Beverly Hills. To an Isa Wolf. "Huh," I thought. In the memo slot was "Loan Repayment." I turned it over. Isa's signature, the Bank's stamp "received" and on the very bottom, in tiny cryptic letters, was "Isa loved Gary very much," exclamation point. "Loved" was underlined three times. Only then I noticed the date – August 21, 1979. Geez, that hit me in the gut.

Way back, I had dated a Jewish man, movie producer, big, big house in the Hollywood Hills, swimming pool, many cars, the rush of waiters when entering Musso and Franks together. You get the picture. He was older, but I really liked him, and we got along. He had a regular house guest, an older woman, whom he said was an old friend in town for medical treatments.

She was so obnoxious and possessive when I met her. I referred to her only as "Pretty in Pink" because of a pastel pantsuit she squeezed her solid 240 lb. frame into. Ridiculous behavior on my part, I know, but it's a girl thing. Any woman worth her salt knows when her man is sleeping with someone.

They were.

Well, one fine day, I noticed a check made out to Malcolm, from her, with nothing in the memo slot. Being suspicious, I asked my best girlfriend her thoughts. "A loan payment, probably," she said. I thought differently. "No, I think he is charging her to stay," I said. "Maybe the sex knocks off a percent or two." My friend was appalled, but I was adamant. Of course I was angry, but I was also very hurt, cut to the quick in fact, and sought retribution. Ok, revenge. I had Pretty in Pink let me in the house when he was at work. "Keep the car running," I told my girlfriend, and proceeded to collect my things. Ah, the beauty of the classic stealth break-up. He didn't realize it for days. Do you suppose I was wrong? Maybe my "salt" was off that day?

That will teach you to always fill in the memo slot!

MY CHICKEN STORY

Jeff Miller

I shot a chicken into the air. It fell to earth somewhere between Culver Boulevard and Washington Boulevard. But then again I couldn't see where it might have landed for sure. Maybe in the hills above Jefferson Boulevard. Or, without any more effort than a push by a single cloud and a good strong breeze, it's still going even now.

It sure made sense at the time. This was a live chicken with widespread, feathered wings for flight and a pointed beak to help it stick wherever it landed. And now without the feathers plucked and the bird being seasoned and chilling in the fridge, the stove and table would be empty of what might have been dinner tonight. But I was raised on dreams of Errol Flynn splitting a yeoman's arrow at the tip and so, with an old bow string and bow, I took up this live chicken that was meant for nothing better than frying or broiling or baking and lofted him into the sky towards a better a place where stories could be told, and legends be made.

Except my wife wanted to know where dinner was when she found the refrigerator empty of all things other than vegetables, tomatoes, peanut butter, ice cream and bottles of vodka and gin in the freezer.

But King Richard was returning from the Crusades, which I don't agree with any more, and Robin Hood, whose role I had offered to myself after many private auditions over the years, was trying to welcome Richard the Lion Hearted back to England or Culver City or whatever world I might have imagined all of us to be in at the time.

"It's the stuff of dreams, Pumpkin," I told my wife, convinced that I was right, "that separates us from savages and gives us reason to believe."

I was hoping she would see the tears falling down my cheeks and appreciate the heart and soul that went into my new way of living in our lost world of today.

"But we don't have anything for dinner!"

She stomped her foot and slammed the door and hadn't understood a word I said.

So I shot a chicken into the air and, where it fell, I knew not where. So I had to go to Ralph's to get a chicken. But I would never go look for the one that got away. I went to Ralph's instead where there are a thousand choices in the cases, some whole, some cut and already washed, not to mention different styles of already cooked ones for me to bring home even though it has been my experience in life that nourishment of the palate will never taste as sweet as dreams made up, or dreams remembered.

But I did forget to bring home dessert.

TREASURES

Marti Rhode

Rising and falling
I danced
On the carousel,
Circling,   Circling,
    Circling,   Circling,   Circling…
      Circling,

always riding
the same faded, white wooden horse,
always wishing to be heard
over the bellowed music,
always reaching
to catch the brass ring,
always grasping nothing
but handfuls of air.

So, I went to Ralph's to get a chicken.

And he was there!
    Basting for tenderness
        Seasoning to keep it fresh
            Creating safe spaces to be heard
                Leading the dance on cold pizza
                    Handing out the brass rings.

It seems that our treasures are to come,
Not from cheap jewelry on endless circles,
But from joy and heart wrapped in jovial packages
of laughter and squirt guns.

Happy Birthday, Jack!

With love from Marti Rhode

THAT DAY

Annabelle Aylmer

The sound of my phone barking woke me from a doze, my scarf over my eyes so

I couldn't see and at first I didn't remember where I was. I smelled smoke and pushing the damp cotton away from my face I wondered where it was coming from. Parked under a large island of canary pines in the lot by Pic 'n' Save, I could see some smoke leaking from a covered trash barrel next

to the dumpster and the smell flashed me to last week when we

Went up the trail behind Ralph's house. We had passed a picnic area where a little tower of grey smoke rose from the grill. It was that day that I first felt the catch near my sternum and suspected that it was more than just a bit of pollution or extra pollen in the air. Amongst the leavings of this careless group of nature lovers had been their wine cooler boxes that smoldered in a heap. The shiny linings burnt with a particular smell that I was terrified of and found difficult to describe. The complex odors of manufacture, burning metal, waxed paper and with a dash of plastic thrown in, it always instantly irritated my lungs and made it hard to breathe. I always got so angry. As well as my lungs feeling raw, I was so offended that people would not pick up after themselves. I didn't know if my judgment of others or my personal injury made me crankier. My dad had been in the navy and a being a bit militaristic seemed a way

to cope with his rambunctious troop. When we went camping, and it was time to pack up, there was a key chain of tasks that would leave the spot more shipshape than we found it.

On that particular day we were climbing on the trail behind

Ralph's house, up the hillside that overlooked the beach. I was aware of the cool cut of the fog and that was when I had felt a sharp tingle in my chest and knew that it was different. I had tried not to

Buy into Ralph's depression, which enveloped him in

a cloud of downer energy. Afterwards in the bathroom, looking up into the mirror and seeing the grit in the

Chicken tracks at the corners of my eyes as I coughed and coughed and coughed that I knew. That it was time to see the doctor.

The brick wall behind the Pic 'n' Save cast a shadow over the dumpster and its rancid contents. I heaved a sigh as I fumbled in the clutter of my bag for my phone. I saw the Dr.'s office number and sighed as I hit the talk button. My office keys fell into the dark between the car seats with a clatter.

"Hello?"

PLAYING CHICKEN

Susan Starbuck

If I had not gone out to Ralph's to look for a chicken
I would have missed Maureen cross-legged
on the pile of playground snow
Dad's tuxedo like a limousine in the closet
An archangel sitting on the piano bench
when Beth played "Clair de Lune"

I would have chickened out, muffled my scream
Avoided Hades, never voiced satire or owned my wit

Now I don't count my chickens easily but believe
There may be a chicken in every pot
I have flown the coop

GO FIGURE

Julie Ariola

He passed in an instant
I ran miles around Washington Square Park
ate dozens of cream puffs from Jon Vie
moved to the land of sunshine and palm trees
a new beginning
Hah!
So I went to Ralph's to get a chicken
And I was home at last

SMORGASBORD

Sheila Young

So I went to Ralph's to get a chicken. It was early, the sun was just starting to rise. In the alley behind my house, blackbirds sat on the telephone wire, black dots against a purple sky. The smell of wet pavement from the midnight rain crept into my heart and made me think of home. I turned on the radio, ACDC blarred from the speakers. I tapped my fingers, one after the other on the porous leather steering wheel. It was hard and cold. I looked up and saw the homeless woman with her dog on the side of the road. She repositioned herself in the brush, her red eyes peeked out from under the hood of her jacket. They glowed with desperation and shot like a laser through my soul. Her dog sat up, shook himself like dogs do and watched me as I drove away. I shuddered as I sped up the alley. Across the empty streets I went and into the empty parking lot of Ralph's. The sun was rising rapidly and I felt the heat through the window. Shards of light danced across the black pavement.

The sliding glass doors parted and I stepped across the threshold. It was cold, I shrugged. My senses were assaulted so early in the morning. I squinted from the fluorescent lights, the ding ding ding of the cash register sounded like a carnival, the smell of homemade bread was intoxicating and the poignant smell of strawberries and peaches through their fuzzy skin felt like summer. Freshly brewed coffee drew me farther and deeper into the store. I looked around and there they were...Chickens sitting in a heated display case, wrapped in plastic and enveloped with a golden glow. It was a smorgasbord of chicken, garlic chicken, lemon chicken, barbeque chicken, teriyaki chicken, fried chicken, baked chicken, chicken wings, chicken legs, chicken breasts, whole chickens, sliced and diced and ready to eat chickens. So many choices. I stood there, saliva pooled in my cheeks and dribbled out the side of my mouth and down my chin. I felt the heat from the case, it felt good so I moved closer. I couldn't decide which chicken to choose. I shifted my weight from side to side and scratched my head. Hmm, keep it simple I told myself. I bit my lower lip and pushed my glasses up the bridge of my nose to get a closer look. So many choices. In the distance I hear a voice, "Go with the Lemon Chicken." I took a deep breath and it occurred to me that it was Jack Grapes! I turned around and there he was, the collar of his polo shirt was turned up and he was clutching on to a bottle of Smart Water. Standing near him was an old man with glassy eyes and a women behind him with a cane trying to get a glimpse into the case of chickens. The line was starting to build. "Jack?" I said, "you really do come to Ralph's to get a chicken?" He smiled and said, "Ah yes, at least once a week."

THE LIST OF JACKS

Roz Levine

The list of Jacks is long and steep
Jack the Ripper brings loss of sleep
Sweet Jack Sprat so good to his wife
Brings on neither anxiety nor strife
There's Jack of quick and nimble fame
And Jacks they named a childhood game
There's good boy Jack, the giant killer
And Jack Daniels, the whiskey distiller
There's Jack Kennedy who's so adored
Killed and Jack Ruby, the one abhorred
There's young Jack and his darling Jill
Who played together on that famous hill
There's our favorite Jack of all the grapes
Who's brilliant, funny, has what it takes
He's a teacher, writer, boxer and actor
A modern Renaissance man by any factor
I could say more because he's way ass kickin'
But, I'm headed to Ralph's to get a chicken

SIMPLY TUESDAY

Timothy Giblin

The liver transplant center is on the 3rd floor of 8900 Beverly Blvd.

Strolling that neighborhood can be a guilty pleasure. A curated blur of Leica lenses, Miele kitchen appliances, Bric a brac, Ligne Roset, carpets, and the roar of Lambos. Today tho, my eye stops short of lingering.

I kick my foot to prop the door, and at the top of my breadth pause and pull the handle. I can feel the light weightlessness of the steel bearings that glide the door. It's monolithic stature and satin finish styles a symbiotic pairing of high tech, good proportions and thoughtful design. Just this door by itself belongs in the neighborhood better than I ever did.

The lobby is panelled in dark walnut veneer and punctuated by lit-gold onyx slabs. the floors are stainless with white terrazzo.

A man dressed in purple scrubs carrying a frappuccino with turquoise ear buds slides in behind me as the elevator door closes. We both hit 3. I look at him, but he tucks into his phone. A move, probably well-practiced yet seemingly benign. I shouldn't take it personally. He's enjoying his coffee or music, anyway I don't belong here. I don't belong period. I'm not a part of this beautiful world anymore, I'm on my way out. Feeling self-conscious, I look at my feet and notice the space around them, the space that I'm taking up. I'm happy when the doors to the elevator open to another big room.

My chest fills back up with the terrazzo and mood lighting. I drag my finger along the Italian leather and touch panel controls. I breathe again, filling my lungs with the chilled, sterile air. I can imagine each pristine particle scraped and ionized. My exhale needing to be erased. I sit and gulp a glance at a woman in a chair. her sunken frame occupies only a small portion of the ergonomic seat. Her personal economy is an unpleasant contribution, like a poorly considered detail in a chapel of design. Wow, I'm getting that elevator feeling again and I wish I could just run out. Run past the walnut,stainless and terrazzo. Run and forget about this place and everything I've seen already, but hey I'm not a kid anymore. I can't defy this authority.

I turn back to her. Her lightweight skin slumps on calcified branches too brittle to function long term. Single steps from ash and lime. Her muscles drape like low slung night crawlers. The room fills up with dark flood water, defeating this ramshackle collection of broken pumps. We are steadily being displaced, a gurgling dark over mounds of insoluble earth.

I never knew there'd be days where I just wished it was a Tuesday. Not THE Tuesday or the how many Tuesday's do I have left Tuesday – just Tuesday – a regular old one. The telling your girlfriend "so I went to Ralph's to get a chicken" kind of Tuesday.

CRACKING THE WISHBONE

Evie Sullivan

"Dark is a way and light is a place,
Heaven that never was
Nor will be ever is always true."
          –Dylan Thomas on his birthday.

Feasting on sea fruit and fresh fish
glancing into the firmament for
the brightest star, the Evening Star,
that leads its long way
to the unavoidable darkness.

Then, at once, a rumble in his stomach.
A sharp pain like a million unseen pieces
breaking through the membrane of his flesh.
There is only one birthday wish left:
A wishbone of wild geese loitering around
the mud green pond with the rainbow shore.

So I went to Ralph's to get a chicken.

THE DANCE

Lisa Cheek

I'd go to Ralph's to buy a chicken, but I don't eat chicken. Haven't since that dreadful New Year's Eve, 1988, eating chicken satays out of a stall in Singapore. Thought I was gonna die! Was in the hospital for a few days upon my return to the States.

So.....since I would not be buying a chicken, I'll buy bacon! Who doesn't like bacon? Now there is something I can sink my teeth into. A BLT! with avocado. Perhaps some Lay's potato chips on the side. Maybe a piece of key lime pie? Yum!

I really have to write two pages? Now what? Maybe I should plan dinner or write a grocery list. I'm hungry. Why did Jack have to bring up chicken? What more can I say about something I don't like and won't eat. Maybe tomorrow I will write something of interest or have something to say. I'm pretty sure I don't, but I hope I get father than this.

Why is filling a page so challenging? My life has been about 30 seconds. I think I feel that if it can't be said in 30 seconds maybe it doesn't need to be said. Get to the point, right? I feel like I'm filibustering here. My dogs sit beside me, not feeling the need to have to produce. They just are. Don't have a care in the world. They lick their butts and then lick my face. That's their day. Why is producing two pages important? How about one and a half or maybe I should change the font size? What's my word count now? 270. I'm barely half -way there.

I'm getting a migraine. It's running up the right side of my neck and screaming through my eyeball. Doesn't this mean it's time to stop? Maybe I'm screaming inside, needing to say something on this page, but all that comes forward is resistance. I hope I have more imagination tomorrow. My intention is to write every day, since it's something I've never accomplished before and it is something one needs to do if they want to be a real writer. I get how this is like dancing. People wonder why one continues to go to dance class and it's because I get better every time I go and I can see the progress and I know it's what will happen here if I become as devotional with this as I do with dancing. Commit. Having seen myself as a recovering commitment phobic for years, I need to have a new self-image. One of a committer.

And since I have not been able to commit to daily writing, perhaps I just need to read a dictionary ever so often, to improve my vocabulary. Will that give me more to say? I feel like four letter words have been my choice in the past. Maybe it's time to move on to 5 letter words. I'm now at 496. Done for today.

FINGER HUT

Jeff Newman

Ralph's

So find

Delivers   crux

                              I   "

a

                    reset   my
         ego
                              get   weigh itself
    elders
                              THE THING
went   democracy   leaves   quest
      with   crash   arid
            flagon the   nature
            to   sings
      planet   collapse
      to   hop   *alabaster*

                                                   paradise

                    patriarchy
         cohesion

                                          chicken
         origami   Zero   edits
            life

THIS IS LA

MK Smyth

After all and it's dinnertime and I have to go to Ralph's to get a chicken a short drive from my house on a cul de sac street just past a neighbor's pink Pitti Palace. A replica now being rented for a year's wages for a week of filming at their swell manse. Other neighbors and dog walkers rerouted through a corridor of industry sprung at the curb last night – film equipment on trolleys and giant white trucks on either side of the street, movie people huddled with the look of "cool" written all over them – running hither thither –dressed in black, their headphones and mics and smartphones engaged; security staff at vantage points and cops in cop cars snooze on standby.

I wait for a few minutes as a crew with a rolling cardboard scrim of minarets crosses in front of my car near a blacked-out talent van, can see a glimpse between vehicles of what my neighbor's place would look like if it were in Seville, Corsica or Istanbul surrounded by food service, trailers, props and turbo generators. With enough cable to light up the sky. Palm trees lighted just so, tilted just so. Cement, stucco and lawns dusted with Swarovski crystals just so a line of actors now walking down a path will glow.

The actors made up "Valentino vaselinos" and "Scheherazades." Swarthy in turmeric tan make-up, their hair – dark, parted, pressed and pomaded in rivulets and pompadours, dressed in colorful costumes – embroidered tunics and flowing silk pants. Ready for action, a parade led by docile leopards on leashes. The vista, a scene from a borrowed coin, a souvenir brought back to surface from the Mediterranean back to LA. A city of island-cities spit-issued to stilled seas known as freeways. Freeways leading to outer cities named for saints, beer, or awkward prettiness – Monica, Corona, Irwindale. No room for a mailman and mom sitting bumper-to-bumper at a tertiary tributary. Strangers playing chicken until someone blinks. I blink and let the postman pass, then turn left, then left, then left again, then drive straight into the sinking sun. At the store I look for a cart and notice the sunset. A faint moon rising. Old lovers who've let the old wars go. Who pretend it's the first time. I watch how they hold each other, lips in a cherish, skin over skin, her throat reddened by his five o'clock shadow, light dimming, her dimpled thigh falling over his hairy leg. Their lovemaking continues until she forgets her name, that she wanted more, that he only gives in fractions – slivers, quarters, halves, or too much, or nothingness but is always there. As for her, she's all fire and wonder this girl. That she chose this life and this man and would do so time again. After all what is time or measure or reason where there is billion-year vapor? The moon knows this and that. And that she has to rove. That she'll be back once she's had her day. It is then when he steps up into the night drinks moonshine with a good gouda and good friends. Bring it on! He says to the stars. The Big Dipper pulls dinner from her pot – Coq au Vin a Jacques. The moon pulls up a chair and asks, Did I tell you the one about the chicken and Ralph's?

(REVERSE)

James Zukin

So I went to Ralph's
And got a chicken
Only to find Chechins
No chickens! Chicken
hearts! Rubbery
chickens Chicken
Littles! Chicken
prompts ... But no
Chickens
Or cooked goose
Posing as a chicken

Just a note
From Madrid Marley
So I ask ask the manager
For Chicken Poems?
Poems for Chickens?
I chickened out
Thinking the reverse
I went to the poetry
On aisle three
And bought some
Conceit
With reverse
Wrapped around it
Here it is:

(Reverse)

THE INIMITABLE MR. GRAPES

Jody B. Fay

Write like you talk, that's what *Jack* says
Find your *3 voices* and *write like you talk*
Beware of adverbs, they're taboo
Drop a 5-er in the kitty if you make a booboo
Massage transformation lines, Book-End Image Moments
Remember that a *Prop* is an essential scene component

Write like you talk in the journals you keep
If inspiration fails you, don't lose sleep
Do what *Jack* says, fill a page with *blah, blah, blah*
Or his favorite finger lickin' *"I went to Ralph's to get a chicken"*
Don't forget a *Prop - there was a penny on the floor*
Ideas will likely surface on your way home from the store

Write like you talk, *Method Writing* pulls the strings
Unleash the creativity that's been waiting in the wings
Follow *Jack's* directions and read all of Chapter 6
After reading Chapter 6, re-read Chapter 6
Be prepared to answer questions about Chapter 6
It might be a good idea to re-read Chapter 6

Write like you talk, that's what *Jack* says
Free fears and insecurities trapped inside your head
Sweep the decks and join the ranks of *Jack's* list of disciples
Spots are filling fast, so grab a seat while you're still able
Classes push and challenge but the end result is big
Jack Grapes awakens writers to express, to thrive – to live

WHEN YOU CAN'T GO TO RALPH'S TO GET A CHICKEN

Marilee Burton

I had a difficult writing week. I had no ideas. Or, to be more accurate, I was resistant to writing as I'm sure there were at least 92 things about which I could have written (including Sweepee Rambo, the blind Chinese Crested Chihuahua who hails from my town, VAN NUYS, and just won the 'World's Ugliest Dog' title. (Her contest entry read: *I'm the prettiest little blue eyed Chinese Crescent Chihuahua he [owner Jason Wurtz of VAN NUYS] has ever known. He loves my baby soft freckled skin and legendary blond Mohawk but most of all he loves my loyalty to him.*)

I should have done the reasonable thing and gone to Ralph's and got a chicken. But it was too hot to go out. Plus, we had Costco chicken thighs in the freezer. So, I did the next best thing. I defrosted the thighs and made chicken salad.

It was delicious! (And now I have something to write about.) Here's the recipe. (All amounts are intuitive, so only ingredients and steps included):

1. Lightly poach chicken thighs
2. Once cool, chop into bit size pieces and put in a bowl
3. Add to the chicken in bowl:
      Celery coarsely chopped
      Tart apple chopped (from backyard Anna apple tree if possible)
      Scallions thinly sliced
      Fresh rosemary minced (from backyard veggie garden if feasible)
      Parsley finely chopped
      Lemon juice (from lemons picked from backyard tree if available)
      Kosher salt
      Raisins
      Dijon mustard
      Miracle Whip
4. Stir
5. Eat
6. Write

HAPPY EASTER

Megan Welch

Morning frost permeated my pale skin,
spread a clammy chill not unlike
the feel of a corpse.
I wanted to persuade myself
that eggs mean life
and chickens lay eggs
so chickens mean life.
But the goat kept on bleating.
So I went to Ralph's to buy a chicken,
but on the way I found a dime
stuck in a crack in the sidewalk,
its silvery edge worn shiny.
I wiggled it loose with two fingers,
rubbed away the dirt,
tried to read the date,
but remembered I'd forgotten my glasses,
remembered I had to hurry,
remembered I had to buy that chicken,
had to stuff it with corn,
had to see the egg it might lay,
I had to know that life was worth living!
But it was 6:15.
Ralph's gates were locked.
Bags of unsold sod and feed piled high.
I could hear the chickens clucking.
I imagined them scratching through gravel
for corn I'd never feed them,
imagined them sold to slaughter,
imagined their cold, plucked thighs,
imagined the eggs they'd never lay, and I knew
beyond all doubt
that chickens are the daughters
and mothers of life.

THE CHICKEN

JOHN C. SMITH

"I went to Ralphs to get a chicken, but did I forget something?" Simon said to himself as he placed the bird on the dining table. "What a magnificent bird you are," he declared.

Cooking was a passion something that gave purpose and meaning to his life.

He desperately wanted to start cooking straight away but he had a dinner appointment with a girl he had met online. During the date he was distracted, all he could think about was the chicken and the dish he was going to prepare.

Finally he returned home. He opened the door and walked in. The chicken was gone. He dashed franticly around the house looking for it but it was well and truly gone.

Who would break into my home and steal my chicken? It just didn't make sense. He considered calling the police but the thought of saying the words "my chicken has been stolen" was too much for him. He could feel his skin breaking out in hives, which it always did whenever he was stressed.

Unable to sleep he decided to take a walk in the nearby park. Darkness fell as he walked fitfully around the perimeter, a lone figure in the moonlit night. Reaching a corner, he noticed a van pull up in front of a house on the opposite side of the street. He watched as two men jump out and start to unload. They removed various pieces of furniture, boxes, and a chicken.

"My God!" Simon exclaimed, "That's my chicken!"

He continued to watch as the men finished unloading and take everything inside the house and close the front door.

Simon could feel his heart racing and sweat breaking out on his brow. 'Shall I call the police?' he thought to himself. 'But what if they don't believe me?' No he concluded I'd rescue the chicken himself.

He crossed the road and noticed a side entrance to the house. The door was unlocked. He opened it and followed the path-way to the back of the house. Through the kitchen window he could see his bird sitting on the kitchen table.

He opened the door and walked in and picked up the chicken.

"What do you think you are doing?" said a voice from the corner of the room.

"This is my chicken and I'm taking it back."

The owner of the voice took out a gun and said in a heavy Russian accent. "I don't think so. Sit down"

Simon placed the chicken back down on the table and obeyed.

Well dear reader, you're probably wondering what happens next to our intrepid hero? Well not only did Simon survive but he went on to cook a magnificent chicken dish for that band of crooks that very night. He rose to become the mob's favorite chef regularly cooking up a culinary delight after a good night of thieving.

Hence the saying - 'Keep your eye on your chicken. You never know where it might lead you."

NO ONE CAME

Eileen Wesson

How about that funeral
No one came
Act three
Last scene
You played to an empty house
That must have hit you when you saw that one
Yeah you were fast funny and fearless
Your scripts
Had happier endings
Than this.
No sweet pillow talk here.
When I heard you died
You left me no choice
 So I went to Ralph's market
And
Got a chicken.

WAITING...

Margaret York

It was dark in the corner of the house and I approached it with trepidation. I had been there before. "Ouch!" I swore as I tripped over the uneven threshold. I could smell it but I knew that it was only my imagination that brought it into my consciousness. If I could only find the note, I thought. I began to move my hands over the top of the table. It was not there.

I went to the window, seeking light. As I pulled back the shade a stream of unfiltered sunshine streaked across the floor. It was not enough light to illuminate the room but it did leave a stripe down the middle of the floor. I got down on my hands and knees. Crawling around, I felt like a child.

I know how to search. I know how to find any object if it is here. My instincts told me it was. I plotted a grid. Factoring in my size and the size of the room I knew I could cover it within eight to ten minutes. I looked at my watch. It was exactly 5:45, well into the hour when most families would be home with their loved ones, preparing dinner, talking about the events of their day. I wanted that for myself. I wanted it for my family.

Starting in the northeast corner of the room I moved in increments. I focused to the left of me and then to the right as I vacated that space. Left, right, move. Left, right, move. I kept this up until I reached the west side of the room, then moved back one space and repeated what I had just done only this time moving to the east. I handled it all with precision. But in the end, there was no note.

I heard a noise coming from the foyer. I made a mental note of just how the furniture was arranged in this crowded space. I needed to go in there but I was not willing to go blindly. Time was running out and I knew it. Soon it would be six o'clock. The foyer looked like a horror movie set. Old dark antique furniture was arranged in such a way that made searching difficult. The noise had come from our old dog, Randy, as he waited at the front door. His tail was hitting the sideboard as he wagged it back and forth aimlessly.

I began by looking over every inch of the side table where the family mail was stacked daily. Then, as I approached the armoire, I saw a small piece of white paper lying on the floor, just in front, as though it had been accidentally dropped there. My heart began to pound as I picked up the note and opened it. "Jack, I went to Ralph's to buy a chicken. Be home soon. Love you, Lori." Thank God. Dinner.

HAPPY ENDINGS

Cheryl Montelle

During the summer
All I wanted to eat was watermelon
Sometimes I ate it plain
Sometimes with salt
Sometimes with feta cheese
The sweet and savory so juxtaposed
As the flesh of the fruit burst and spread
Between my tongue and roof of mouth

Then one day as happens every year
Summer ended and it was time to get serious
So I went to Ralph's to get a chicken
To celebrate the end of languid evenings
Filled with Milky Way skies

GREEN EYED MONSTER

Olivia Schwartz

I was 16 the winter I got my license. The day was in January, winter, but not of the unbearable kind of winter. This was San Francisco… cold, but doable, no snow, no bitter days of huddling inside my coat—a warm sweater, always my green one that matched the eye shadow I wore. Mr. Gibbs, my science teacher, called me the green-eyed monster – I did like to put on a thick layer.

Girls in those years dressed up for school, we wore our hair in curlers at night. *Seventeen* magazine taught us how to sleep on them. My pain was in the superficiality of it all and yet I had not a clue.

The suburbs of San Francisco were different from the suburbs of New York. I grew up very protected, but aren't all children?

I remember sitting in our den, specially designated for the T.V. I didn't like watching, I was always a little odd, but I loved my family and so that is where we sat together in the evenings.

"Livvy, please bring me my slippers," my father said. My father's feet were resting on the brown leather ottoman, the one I have as a memory today. My father was meticulous in his dress and his person and I tried to be the opposite. He was 5'8", medium-weight, bald head, and always wore black glasses and a warm smile when he looked at me. The den, his favorite room, much smaller than our large living room and dining room, was the room we used, we sat in, and shared in and I grew in. The T.V. was large, a big presence in our communal life—Perry Como, Ed Sullivan, golf tournaments and the news. The news was confusing to a young girl, a girl from the Five Towns who only knew plenty and good and love and kindness.

The T.V. announcer was anxious, the pictures were of young black children being attacked, yelled at, intimidated by big burly white adults screaming at them. The civil rights movement was in full force and I didn't know what I believed. I was young. I remember in my being, in my soul, hoping and praying for direction, but I knew the direction I believed in, did my father believe the same? The window was open and my brother placed his favorite scare-toy on the windowsill, a plastic, black widow spider. He liked to hear me scream.

I was holding my breath, waiting for my dad to speak, but I only saw tears streaming down his face. He felt the pain of these children being mistreated and I felt relief. "We are of the same heart," I said aloud. My father turned to me and smiled.

I was filing through my memories as I waited for my mother to come home. I was sixteen and a day and I wanted the car. I wanted to drive thru A-1 Root Beer like all the other cool kids. I wanted my freedom, I wanted to run my life. However, my mother thought differently. What was to be my first outing solo, my first driving experience I will never forget? "No, you can't mean it," I said to my mom. "Yes," she said. "This is the only thing I will give you the car for." And so I went to Ralph's and bought a chicken. When I came home my mom said, "Enough driving for your first time out." I was not happy about that and so at dinner, I refused to eat that chicken.

MR. POET

Florence Murry

I go to Ralph's to buy a chicken
& ran into Jack Grapes.
He is there to buy a chicken.
I tell him how much I liked his poem,
"Any Style" in the latest *Rattle Magazine*.
LA poet for sure.
500 miles to go
to white sand beaches
his twilight lit eternal diner
his waitress ready for the order,
his boundless coffee like mud.
We have been there.

Just keep those poems coming
any style, Mr. Poet.
Tonight I will have my chicken,
any style,
side of gravy
side of mashed potato
side of cranberry sauce
LA style.

–from "Any Style" Jack Grapes, *Rattle #52 Summer 2016*

ET CETERA

Catherine Kaufman

I grew up with a dictionary at the kitchen table. It was my President Mother's idea. She wanted my brother and reporter me to learn as many words as possible. One morning I asked her horses what the word *riveted* meant. She gave me her standard milk answer which was, "Look it up." Oh Jack-o-lantern, why did I even bother to ask. So I looked it up and witches didn't understand the definition very well until years later when I saw Yul Bryner on Broadway newspaper in *The King & I*. Watching him strut back and forth across the stage declaring, "et cetera, swing et cetera, et cetera," I was crown riveted and finally understood the true dictation meaning of the word. I loved the idea of spouting words and having someone else write them down. Right then I vowed that one day I would have a yellow secretary. And the first words I would say would be, "So I went to Ralph's to get a purple chicken."

PUT A RING ON IT

Matthew Hetznecker

I try to open my eyes, my head rebels, Ouch! Well I drank too much. I squeeze one eye open, look at the clock, 11:30 a. m., God I hope— yes its Saturday! What happened?! I remember a text—Francis. "We're going out, early. I got a surprise!" Then emojis (there was a uncorked champagne bottle and a stunned face)— Celebration!—I did shots, three?—before I left— no driving —LYFT—where did we met?

Something brushes my leg, I jerk up and look over to the other side of the bed. Shit! There is a nest of brown hair on one of my pillows.

OK—think, try thinking—-that's not working—I pull the sheets off me, they tear at my belly. Ouch—OK—a big load and, no shower. I slide my foot out—there's an onion ring on my second toe, left foot—OK—Jack-in-the-Box. I lift the sheets a bit more—G-string, purple lace—did I pay for play?! No I gave that up.

I put a foot on the floor and pull the onion ring off, I glance at my bed mate, she moves, turns her head to me, her face is covered in a brown mess, I see closed eye, lots of black-smeared mascara. OK, she's from out on the town? Oh please be, out-of-town-fun-girl. I look for more clues near the bed without getting up. There's a red t-shirt under the nightstand. Hers. OK, where are her pants? Hmm—anything—jeans? I pick up the T-shirt—Fuck! It's a dress, a tiny red dress. I now remember pulling this off.

I sit up, What's that? Something sparkles in the mid-morning sun on the wood floor next to my yellow sport brief. SHIT! It's one of those crown things—tiara, for a bachelorette party, I reach to turn it over—she better be, "Maid OF—NO!

Bride To BE."

OK, calm down. I peek at my bed mate. At a church? No! A bar, THE ABBEY! Clues? More clues—My phone. Francis! I grab my phone, off the nightstand. OK, text—from Francis. A few!

Your (coffin) you Dick!
You passed out you idiot!
I'm downstairs! Answer your fuckin buzzer!
Where are you? WTF?!
Call me! (ten texts)
My sister is not answering, I'm worried, is she with you?
The girls said you left with her.
Where is Kylie?
Where are you and my sister? The girls said you left awhile ago.
On my way! CU

"FUCK, FUCK, FUCK," I whisper.

Kylie stirs. "Hmmmm," she says.

I can't make it at 4 p.m. OK, my sister is in town for her bachelorette party. They're at The Abbey, starting early! Her name is Kylie, you'll find her, I also text you her #. Tell her take it slow. There wasn't any stuff /food at my place so I went to Ralph's to get a Chicken. CU AAYF!

APPROACHING THE SUMMER SOLSTICE

Barbara Moreno

The first week of June
I remembered how Jack insisted
we take the summer to fill ourselves up.
So when I found myself stuck in Skokie
I slid past my analytical hour
into a taxi headed for Chicago
and stumbled up the museum's marbled steps
searching for images of Buddhas
I could breathe in and out of,
faces I could stow away home.

The next week of June
I remembered Jack when I handed
the school's art teacher yet another banker's box
of brightly patterned shoulder pads, the collections my mother
had lined up in rows and columns before she died.
The school's youngest children had cupped them into ears
for the masks of jaguars and foxes and bears
they hid their secret selves behind.
And then I told the teacher Jack's cautionary tale
about taking the summer to fill herself up.

And the week after that,
when summer got serious in Los Angeles,
I remembered Jack when I peered
into my refrigerator trying to patch together
a meal from the scraps lodged
in the cartons of leftovers.
He had always told us, "Never write a poem
on an empty stomach."
so I went to Ralphs to get a chicken
to write a poem about.
It turned out to be the only sensible thing
I could do in order to fill myself up.

THAT OLE WHITE MAGIC

Isabel Brome Gaddis

I went to Ralph's to get a chicken. I was taking an online class ("Voodoo for White Women Who Hunger for a Spiritual Connection That Does Not Deny the Body, But Who Have Enough Awareness of Cultural Appropriation Not To Try This Shit In Public") and I needed the bones.

"I need a chicken with a little 'oomph' to it," I said to the guy behind the meat counter.

He moved to a row of organic fryers and gave each a pat. He pulled two.

"This guy's got a lot of oomph," he said, holding up a small fryer in his left hand. "But I think this one's more authentic," he said, lifting a larger chicken with his right.

I wished I had read ahead in the class notes. "I don't want an inauthentic chicken," I said, "but I do need the oomph."

"You pays your money and you takes your chances," he said.

I fingered the teal micro-suede gris-gris bag hanging around my neck and waited for guidance. The big chicken seemed showy. But what if the little guy was all bluster and no content?

I noticed a row of stuffed cornish game hens.

"How about those?" I asked.

"You have a good eye," he said. "Stuffed with wild rice, porcini mushrooms, and sage. Martha Stewart described the recipe as 'mellow and earthy.'"

I'm old enough to remember when Martha was the voodoo queen of my people. You don't have to hit me over the head with spiritual guidance.

"I'll take that one," I said, pointing. While he wrapped up my bird, I said, "Are they really from Cornwall?"

"Would you be disappointed if they came from Connecticut?" he said.

Another sign. "If I were wearing them, I would clutch my pearls," I said. "I feel the support of my ancestors."

"You and me both, kid," he said, handing over the bird.

I wanted to thank him for his help with my spiritual development, but there was a woman standing by the pork roasts, so I let him go.

As I walked toward the cash register I felt the bird's tiny dead wings through the butcher paper, and said to myself, "I need the bones. I need the bones. I need the bones."

SOME THINGS NEVER CHANGE

Barbara Rothstein

Over time, the moss on the north side
of the blue fir tree in our backyard
reached out and crawled around
my daughter's little wrought iron chair.
The toy chair remained there,
leaning against the tree for years,
tilted in union until it became
a mossy extension of the tree,
as if attached to the tree,
like Roger and I were attached
attached to that dreamy wooded acre
of our first house, attached to our youth,
our child an extension of us.

As she grew from a baby, to a girl,
to a young woman,
her tears mingled with mine
hundreds of times. Now,
it's because her father has stopped breathing
forever. Yet when death surprised him,
leaving a last dark spurt of mucous
on the side of his mouth, it was she,
who without a beat of hesitation,
had wiped it away. Always meticulous,
he would have been ashamed,
though he's beyond that now.

But I was ashamed,
ashamed that my daughter was the one
who had done that for him
with so little effort
and so much tenderness,
ashamed that I was the one
who had let that awful drool sit there,
letting it burn its way
into my mental gallery

of never-to-be-forgotten images.

So I went to Ralph's and bought a chicken.
Then I bought an onion.
I bought two leeks. I bought three parsnips
I bought six carrots. Last,
I bought a small bunch of dill for seasoning
and I made chicken soup for all our souls.

NO HOME WORK

Karla Kuester

It's unexpected. But due to cancellations, I'm home today. I move through the apartment like a sleepwalker. There are things I'm pressed to do. The litter of unpaid bills on the table, a bag of recycling to take to the bin, a pile of unhung shirts, a list of phone calls to return, emails to send, junk mail to shred, a sink full of dishes.

But I don't wanna do it. Any of it. It doesn't matter what I choose. I'm tired. I'm resistant. It all feels like homework.

I just wanna sit here on my bed, pressed into the solid contraption of my overstuffed pillows and close my eyes. A vision of my inbox with the 12 words that say 'new' appears. It morphs into a page of two and three-digit addition, subtraction, multiplication, and division equations from my fourth grade text book in the hard spot behind my eyes. Home work. It all feels like homework. And I don't wanna do it.

"That's life!" A cruel voice tears a dark shard in the back of my mind. I manage a "Shhhh" to quell the voice and pictures.

I just wanna sit here and listen to the neighbor's shower that falls like rain, the crunch and hiss of the cars in the alley, the breeze as it clack through the blinds and turns my arms to gooseflesh.

I just wanna sit here feeling the sinews and debits of my spine, the basket of my ribs, the corners of my hips, the tissues around my bones. I just wanna sit here and feel all 10 toes, my hair and fingernails grow, the air of each breath released on my upper lip.

Some might call it boredom.

Some might call it the doldrums.

Some might call it hormonal imbalance.

Some might call it a planetary problem.

Some might call it midlife crisis.

I'm not anxious or depressed, just sort of flat. Resting my attention, my desire. Watching with an open heart, waiting for the next best thing to happen.

Yesterday I went to Ralph's and got a chicken. She's waiting too, in the cool dark womb of the refrigerator. Because I'm not hungry and cooking also feels like homework. And I don't wanna do it.

TELEMACHUS

Debra Franco

Lately plump Chuck Nelligan came from the Stairmaster, bearing a bowl of quinoa on which a carrot and a radish lay crossed. A yellow hoodie, branded with the name of his gym, was sustained gently behind him in the moist air from the men's shower. He held the bowl aloft and intoned:

— *Introibo ad altare Ralphi.*

Winded, he peered down the dark Stairmaster and called crossly:

—*Come up, Kinch. Come up, you out of shape pussy. I can't take one more day of this. I need protein and I need it now. You've got to go to Ralph's and get me some chicken!*

JUNE 6, 2016
PITTENWEEM, FIFE
SCOTLAND

Kathleen Matson

Dear Jack,

It's been 18 years, longer than either of my marriages. Of course we aren't in *that* particular - *WAY* particular - bubble together, but a writing bubble

of our love of literature....

and your four simple rules:

write like you talk

transformation line

massage the transformation

image moment.

OK. Sure.

I want to write you something memorable.

I want to write

I want to fabric girdle, to fish fry, the hurry up to wait - just get a chicken, just run wild, just daffodil my guts out all the while you sit there, at the kitchen table, Jesse at your feet, Lori with her head in the refrigerator, Josh at the piano, sit there with the LA Times in your hands and look up,

and smile

'cause you get hold out, in an ancient sort of way…

Thank God I know you.

Thank you.

I am so glad you are here, on the planet.

You didn't make me good, but you made me better.

When the wings get close and take us,
little by little we will all be there,
tipping the guy with the pizza,
arranging the snacks,
the ac on and off
with you, the whole phantasmagoric rigmarole -
smiling
everlasting
everlasting
you.

Happy Birthday Jack, again and again and again.

Love,
Kathleen Matson

SQUEAMISH

Holly O'Meara

So I went to Ralph's to get a chicken. I'm shopping these days for my elderly parents, and they've given me a list. As a lifelong vegetarian, I wasn't going to cook one, that's for sure. A rotisserie bird for me, double-bagged in case it leaks.

Once, when I was a young adult living at home, I cooked a bird in spite of my distaste for meat. The oven has stopped working on Thanksgiving Day. My parents don't know who to ask for help in their rural neighborhood, so I phone my best friend from Junior High School. Jen rents a room in a house about a mile away. Yes, the oven is available. My mom has prepped the turkey, that gross business of pulling out tendons and unpacking the squishy organs. I load the corpse, the pan, and the baster into my stick shift Mazda painted by Earl Scheib, and head out.

Jen's going into town later for a meal at her mom's. Didi, the owner of the house, is about to leave for seafood at the Beach Café with her daughter, Sarah, on holiday from college.

"Sarah, this is my friend," Jen introduces me. Sarah is a pale teen with tendrils of dyed red hair around her face. She's wearing a cream colored slip, army boots, eyeliner, and a butterfly tattoo. Behind her, a carpeted stairway climbs through space. A coffee table is piled with books, and a bicycle leans against the wall. The kitchen is clean, cleaner than ours. On the table lies a black and orange cocktail napkin. There's a smell of Pine-Sol Lemon Fresh.

Sarah drops to her stomach and launches at me in a combat crawl. Before I can react, she grabs my leg with both hands and bites me on the ankle. She exits with Didi while Jen tries to explain. "Sorry about that. Sarah's a little strange. She's—a performance artist."

Jen helps me cook, and I return to my parents' house, providing a turkey I won't eat. A handful of family members await me. Rarely are outsiders included in our holidays. On this mission, I've orbited out from home base, and made it safely back. I've broken through the barrier of my quirky, insulated family. My table got bigger that year. I learned that other families are strange, too. There was a kind of intimacy in Sarah's greeting, as if she knew me well enough to clasp her teeth in me, play with me, challenge me. Although I responded with shock, a part inside was thawing, expanding its raw veggie edges.

I roll down the windows of the car, so I don't have to smell the chicken. This is performance art, after all. The wind stirs me, the parts inside that want to bite back, play, challenge myself. I drive the chicken home.

NOT OK, CUPID

Ellie Feldman

Some guys would suck the marrow
right out of your bones, if you let them.
How do I know this?
Well, let's just say
there are red flags along the way.
So this evening, after I emailed…

"Dear Stanley,
It was a wonderful two-week love affair,
during which you were the consummate gentleman,-
generous,
witty,
and so much fun to be with,-
however, after deep reflection
following your two-hundred and twenty-three-minute phone call tonight
fifteen days after we met,
proposing marriage and insisting
that I would be a stupid fucking bitch
if I refused to accept and be yours exclusively
until death do us part
because money was no object
and you could give me everything I ever wanted
and more
much more
much, much, more than I ever dreamed possible–
a phone call, during which
I managed to insert exactly five sentences–
it is now clear
beyond the need for any further conversation,
that we are on divergent paths
and it will not work for me to continue this relationship.
I wish you only the best in your life."

…Well, I found my own self
in a marrow-sucking mood,
so I went to Ralph's to get chicken.

INSIDE HIS CHICKEN

Lucienne Lane

He asked me over to his place.
Me, the one who still knows nothing
about cocktails
or how to be.
We drank Dark and Stormies.
He talked, I listened
from the kitchen
to the living room
to the bedroom
and back to the kitchen.
Between the broccolini
and lemon sorbet
something about a sweet girl
ending in a big fight,
the one we never had.
He talked, I yawned.
Driving home I felt nothing
so I went to Ralph's to get a chicken
the one on 3rd and La Brea
where my people go
and deserted shopping carts
wait to be claimed
by new and capable hands.
I guess I dodged a bullet
but if he asked me back tomorrow
who knows
I might just spread my wings
and fly into uncertainty
again.

CHICKENLESS

Marley Klaus

So I went to Ralph's to get a chicken but, when I got there, all the chicken was gone. I mean, the case was there, the labels said this brand and that brand with little bar codes underneath so you know they weren't messing around, cause there's nothing more true, more not-messing-around than a bar code but, well, nothing. Not a pale pink breast, not a set of dismembered thighs, not one Styrofoam container in the case. And I thought, how could this be? Had there been a run on chicken? A gobble-up? An APB I missed? A warning? Disease? Recall? Because, like, Ralph's was made of chicken. All chicken, all the time. Never a chickenless Ralph's. Not a chance. Couldn't be.

"Maybe this isn't Ralph's," I said to myself.

And then I said, "Marley," I liked my name so I always used it when I talked to myself. "Marley," I said, "you've done this before, gotten so wrapped up in the yak-yak in your head, that you've walked into one place thinking you were somewhere else. Maybe you've done it again."

Now, don't get me wrong, I know it's the most ordinary, everyday sort of thing to do, to end up in the wrong car, wrong house, wrong airport, wrong bed. I, like, did it all the time. I mean, who hasn't? So the empty case/wrong store didn't twist my nips. Nah, I just turned right around and marched back up the aisle, the one that was supposed to have chicken in it, turned at the balloons and carnations, then again at the stacked charcoal and lighter fluid, and then to the front door but, guess I must have walked too fast for those personal reactor sensors cause the doors didn't budge, didn't so much as shudder when I walked up to them.

"Marley," I said, "Not your day." I didn't add "girl" because that kind of sass I didn't have. Never did. I was stuck in some nether region between 'girl' and 'woman', one that had no word for it. Maybe that's the reason I liked my name so much. I just couldn't broaden out my category from there.

But the yak-yak nailed it: it wasn't my day. I mean, there I was, trapped in Ralph's/not Ralph's cause I tried to get a chicken when I couldn't even stand to look at it on display, the grocery spotlights on those pimpled places where the feathers got yanked, you know those open pits like already-popped zits, all mashed up against the plastic you could never get your fingers through? Made me want to heave, like, massive chunks. I'm telling you, I could do it right now just giving you the blow-by-blow. But, like I said, I went to Ralph's to get one anyway, because that's what I do, I do stuff anyway. I do stuff I don't want to do, like, all the time. Put me next to someone who wants chicken, who wants chicken without the work, an effortless fucking chicken and, there I go, getting chicken. I do stuff I don't want to do because I want to, that's how nothing I am. I'm so not there I want to do what I don't want to do if someone else has a want they want, a want they know they want, a want they know they want someone else to do, I'm their girl. Nothing girl.

I was so nothing Not Ralph's door sensors couldn't read me.

Capiche?

Outside the glass doors, pigeons pecked and scuffled over a flattened coffee cup lid in the parking lot, the hard cold sun made metal of their speckled backs. But, with the doors that ignored me, what choice did I have but to turn around and head back for the chicken case, maybe find the chicken manager, the store manager, the God of the Grocery because I needed some answers, I needed some warmth, I needed some release from the chickenless Not Ralph's but, when I turned around I wasn't even in Not Ralph's anymore but in front of a short brick building, a sort of fake colonial – Jack's. Now, this was a door I could handle so I walked up the steps and it, too, wouldn't budge.

I shook it. Rattled it.

Nothing.

No chicken. No Ralph's. And I'd lost my way with doors. All of them, it seemed. On the left there was a keypad. I remember Jack saying something about a code but couldn't for the life of me remember what it was, so I was about to give up when a huge gust of what I thought was wind snapped my hair around my face but this wasn't just any kind of wind. It was a dream that sometimes dreamers dream of a place long ago that never was but might be sometime again soon, where friends can fly and memories soar to a place beyond the reach of the liquid lizard birds and pelicans can lend a hand or a feather or beak and tell a sad tale of what was once and never might be. One after another, these four pelicans flew down and, with a swoop and a call to the young dreamers they once were, pushed "6" and then "5" and then "3" and then the last, a show-off looped-de-loop bird called out, "I'm Rufus, you dufus. The number's the same as the address on the awning, the one you could never remember to forget, when stars dance and fade beneath the light of the moon so far and away!" And then, with a switch of his tail feathers as he pushed off and away, between the sky blue with wonder and the black gray cement sea, above a field of torn lost lotto dreams and stray glistening gems of gum chewed and then spat out, his last act of kind mercy, the push beep of the number "5" and the click of a door quite open to the girl who'd once been nothing until she became something in the warm welcome wind and the carefree rescue of Jeff's beak-bellied friends over Wilshire in flight.

Well, I found out where all the chicken went. There probably wasn't a chicken left in any Ralph's anywhere on the planet. They were all on the food table in Jack's class. Every single person had gone out to Ralph's to get a chicken and brought them in. There was fried chicken, raw chicken, chicken cacciatore, chicken nuggets, chicken parmagiana, coq au vin, chicken marsala, kung pao chicken, chicken and waffles, barbequed chicken, lemon chicken, chicken fried chicken, chicken pot pie, chicken fingers, chicken-lickin', chicken little, chicken noodle soup, chicken & grits, chicken cordon bleu, chicklets, and chicken-flavored chex mix.

But, there I was chickenless. It was like I'd stood up to read an image moment piece with an eye wink between my bookends, or with no answer to "why is an moment not a minute?" or without a prop or, worst of all, with a prop bigger than a hand.

So I turned right back around and went to Gelson's to get a chicken...

Jack wouldn't mind. Jack likes anything.

Except props bigger than your hand.

And people who don't laugh at his jokes.

Marilee Burton, Jules Swales, Suzanne O'Connell
Carolyn Rothstein-Ziel, and Cirelle Raphalian